CW00486232

Sheffield's Most Notorious Gangs

To Alison, who has not only been my biggest fan, my reason for getting out of bed in a morning, and the love of my life; but has also agreed to be my wife. I haven't got a clue where to start telling you how much you mean to me.

Also, to my Mum, Jacqueline, who kindly reprised her role as proof reader and critic, and has been as supportive as only a mother could be from the moment I put my first word to paper; and to my Dad, John, who never fails to provide help and support, whatever the situation.

And to my friend, Trevor Stockbridge, who allows himself to be forcibly pulled into my strange world on a regular basis, and provides the kind of morale boosts that only a good friend can.

Finally, thanks to Joe, Ed, Alexis, Ian, Jessica, Rosie, Charlie, Krysta, John, Billy, Charlotte, Joyce, Jan, Alan, Sue and Simon – Making you all proud is why I do this.

Sheffield's Most Notorious Gangs

Ben W. Johnson

PEN & SWORD
HISTORY

AN IMPRINT OF PEN & SWORD BOOKS LTD.
YORKSHIRE - PHILADELPHIA

First published in Great Britain in 2018 by
Pen & Sword History
an imprint of
Pen & Sword Books Ltd
Yorkshire - Philadelphia

Copyright © Ben W. Johnson, 2018

ISBN 978 1 52670 296 8

The right of Ben W. Johnson to be identified as Author of this work has been
asserted by him in accordance with the Copyright, Designs and Patents Act 1988.

A CIP catalogue record for this book is
available from the British Library.

All rights reserved. No part of this book may be reproduced or transmitted in any
form or by any means, electronic or mechanical including photocopying, recording
or by any information storage and retrieval system, without permission from the
Publisher in writing.

Printed and bound in England
By CPI Group (UK) Ltd, Croydon, CR0 4YY

Pen & Sword Books Ltd incorporates the Imprints of Pen & Sword Books
Archaeology, Atlas, Aviation, Battleground, Discovery, Family History, History,
Maritime, Military, Naval, Politics, Railways, Select, Transport, True Crime,
Fiction, Frontline Books, Leo Cooper, Praetorian Press, Seaforth Publishing,
Wharncliffe and White Owl.

For a complete list of Pen & Sword titles please contact

PEN & SWORD BOOKS LIMITED
47 Church Street, Barnsley, South Yorkshire, S70 2AS, England
E-mail: enquiries@pen-and-sword.co.uk
Website: www.pen-and-sword.co.uk

or

PEN AND SWORD BOOKS
1950 Lawrence Rd, Havertown, PA 19083, USA
E-mail: Uspen-and-sword@casematepublishers.com
Website: www.penandswordbooks.com

Contents

Prologue

The Guns Fell Silent

'Who says that ye are dead, ye Albion sons,
Youth strong in flesh, Olympian in brain,
Who sleep there in France where boom'd the guns,
Near Ypres, Loos, or by the silvery Aisne?'

Sgt John William Streets, Poet and Soldier
(Sheffield City Pals Battalion)

K nee deep in foetid mud, and cowering from the explosions which lit up the Belgian sky; there can be very few situations in which a poet would find themselves less drawn to creating verse. Yet, under these hellish conditions, a number of creative young men found solace in documenting their current plight. As such, this merciless and industrial conflict found itself a group of special witnesses; those who kept their pencils as sharp as their bayonets, and found a noble beauty in every dehumanising moment of this ugly war. Many of us will be familiar with the famous works of poets such as Wilfred Owen, Robert Laurence Binyon, and Siegfried Sassoon, whose powerful works live on in inscriptions carved in stone upon every war memorial across the nation, and whose verse has been studiously examined by schoolchildren and scholars for a century. These men live on in our national psyche, their works being resurrected in every new school year, and on every Remembrance Sunday. In the words of Binyon himself 'We will remember them'.

Yet, this flood of poetic outpouring did not stop with the men who would be immortalised by their beautifully crafted verses. They were joined by a number of lesser known poets, who scratched their thoughts, experiences and feelings into their service notebooks each night, as they cowered from the surrounding chaos in their wet and muddy refuge. The work of these men would prove to be invaluable to the history of this terrible conflict, as this was the truth of war, untouched by the naivety of those who were not there, and undiluted by the newspaper editors with their personal political agendas.

These were the men who lived in hell, and made no exception in detailing the horrors of their current existence. Yet, they also found beauty in the carnage and chaos around them. Their works often hold a unique sense of contrast, as stark as the battle which engulfed them. These were eyewitness testimonies to what men were capable of doing to each other, but also, what men were capable of doing *for* each other. For every casualty and capitulation, there were heroes and camaraderie. Never before had a group of poets captured both extremes of humanity from such close quarters, and in such a personal way.

One such poet, whose work would never receive the plaudits and fame garnered by the works of Owen, Binyon and Sassoon, was a young man who had not received the benefit of an extensive education, yet toiled each day to support his family before using his meagre amount of free time to study poetry and literature. His name was John William Streets and, like Wilfred Owen, would never live to see his work published or appreciated. He was an unassuming Derbyshire man, who answered the call of his country, and witnessed the true horrors of war alongside the rest of his comrades; the Sheffield City Pals Battalion.

Will (as he was known to family and friends) was born on 24 March 1886, in the village of Whitwell, Derbyshire. His parents, William and Clara, were known in the local area as a hardworking and friendly couple, and were regular attendees at the local church, the Whitwell Wesleyan Chapel. Their eldest son was a credit to his parents, and proved to be a conscientious student and a talented pianist by the time he reached his teens. The family home of 16 Portland Street would, however, become something of a crowded environment, as Will was to be the eldest of twelve children.

It may have been this over-population in the Streets' residence that would eventually lead Will away from his promising educational future. At the age of 14, he had been offered a place at the local Grammar School, but chose to leave full time education, and from the age of 14, to his late twenties, he toiled each day at the coal face of the Whitwell Coal Mine. His wages provided a much-needed boost to the family income, and was greatly appreciated by William and Clara, who were only too aware that, in more favourable circumstances, their son could have enjoyed a very different life.

It is testament to the character of Will Streets that he bore no grudge towards his parents, and was more than happy to take on the responsibilities of providing for his younger siblings. His hardworking outlook on life was also reflected by the fact that he chose to continue his education in his precious free time, spending his evenings studying French and Classics.

He had hired the services of a tutor, John Mills, which also came from his meagre wages. Mills would eventually become something of a mentor to Will, and was only too happy to provide more tuition than Will could pay for, seeing in his student a rare talent with an infectious eagerness to learn.

However, by the time Will reached 28, the world had become a very different place, and the country had been drawn into the conflict which was beginning to spread across Europe. Like many educated men, Will thought the war to be pointless and imperialistic, and even confided in his parents that he found the idea of war in general to be a sickening and brutal affair. Yet, like hundreds of thousands of young men, Will would not turn his back on his country, and wasted no time in travelling the relatively short distance to Sheffield, and signing up to serve in His Majesty's Army. War had only been declared the previous month, and this brave and honest young man was one of the first to answer the call.

On his arrival in the city, he joined a long and rowdy queue at the Sheffield Corn Exchange, eventually reaching the enlisting officer after hours spent chatting and joking with the other men around him. Will was enlisted in the 12th Service Battalion, York and Lancaster Regiment, which was also to be known as the Sheffield Pals Battalion. He was given the regimental number of 12/525, and paused to wait for his new-found friends, who would eventually gather together under a hastily produced sign, which read 'To Berlin – via the Corn Exchange'.

The next fifteen months were spent in various training camps, which included Penkridge and Ripon. Despite his misgivings about the legitimacy of the war which had continued to spread across the continent, and now cast its shadow across the whole world, Will found a natural affinity for life in the armed forces. He wrote to his family regularly, and without any sense of self-pity or fear, often asked his parents to accept the possibility that he may never return home; he was part of an unstoppable event in history, and could only accept the fate that lay before him.

It was during the Battalion's final training camp in Hurdcott, near Salisbury, that Will began to spend time writing his thoughts in a small red leather –bound notebook, thoughts which eventually become poems, which recorded the events experienced by Will and thousands of others. It was whilst at this particular camp that the blossoming poet wrote 'Hymn to Life: Hurdcott Camp', which ends with a striking and staunch verse, hinting at his acceptance of death, and his intention to meet his fate without hesitation:

'I knew that in that hour I shall undaunted stand
With purpose in my eyes, sword in my hand;
I know that when I sink beneath the strife
I there shall dream of Love, exult in Life'

When the time came to leave the training camps, the Sheffield Pals were tasked with joining up with the 31st Division, with whom they would travel thousands of miles to North Africa. Their duty was to be based in Alexandria, Egypt, where they would make up part of the defence force who would protect the Suez Canal from enemy occupation. This was a far cry from rural Derbyshire, but Will Streets continued in his dedication to the battalion and its ultimate goal. However, just two months later, the battalion was on the move again; this time to a battleground which had already become infamous. The Sheffield Pals were being relocated to the Somme.

By the beginning of April 1916, the battalion had arrived, along with the April showers, into a world almost indescribably bleak. They passed the battlefields at a distance, silently reflecting upon the blood and mud soaked abyss which stretched towards the horizon. Their first port of call was to be the training and preparation area which lay close to the dreaded Somme. The two months spent here would be the last experience of basic civilisation for many of the men, as they relentlessly dug practice trenches, worked on their attack formations, and generally acclimatised to the unforgiving world into which they had now been indoctrinated.

The area of the Somme in which the Sheffield Pals would be operating was one of the only wooded areas which remained in the bomb and shellfire battered fields. Made up of four copses, named Matthew, Mark, Luke and John, this particular stretch of land had changed hands several times, and was a key outpost in the wider battle for control of the area. For weeks the men studied the maps and elevation diagrams, until they knew the area like the back of their callused and chapped hands. This continued until the preparation was deemed to be complete, and the men were allowed a few days of rest until a date was set for the attack.

During this period of inactivity, Will Streets once again took to his poetry as a means of escaping the impending events. The verses jotted into his notebook had now taken on a new and emotional tone. There appeared a strong theme of death and finality in his poetry, but as always, no sense of anger or bitterness. The men of the battalion knew what was expected of them, and as such, fate now rested in their own hands. The poems were sent by post to a publisher, Galloway Kyle, accompanied by a letter from Will, which confirmed his acceptance of death, and gave a glimpse into the life he and his fellow soldiers had endured for the last two months.

> 'They were inspired while I was in the trenches, where I have been so busy I have had little time to polish them. I have tried to picture some thoughts that pass through a man's brain when he dies. I may not see the end of the poems, but I hope to live to do so. We soldiers have our views of life to express, though the boom of death is in our ears. We try to convey something of what we feel in this great conflict to those who think of us, and sometimes, alas! Mourn our loss.'

One of the poems which stood out in the collection was entitled 'Matthew Copse'. This was one of the areas which the Sheffield Pals had spent the last months studying tirelessly. However, in testament to his artistic nature and fatalistic beliefs, Streets painted a picture of natural beauty, choosing to concentrate upon the picturesque qualities of the copse, which was once, and would in the future, be an oasis of woodland refuge set into a landscape of seemingly never-ending open fields.

> 'Once in thy secret close, now almost bare,
> Peace yielded up her bountiful largess;
> The dawn dropp'd sunshine thro' thy leafy dress;
> The sunset bathed thy glade with beauty rare.
>
> Spring once wove here her tapestry of flowers,
> The primrose sweet, the errant celandine;
> The blue-bell and the wild rose that doth twine
> Its beauty 'round the laughing summer hours.
>
> Here lovers stole unseen at deep'ning eve,
> High-tide within their hearts, love in their eyes,
> And told a tale whose magic never dies
> That only they who love can quite believe.
>
> Now 'mid thy splinter'd trees the great shells crash,
> The subterranean mines thy deeps divide;
> And men from Death and Terror there do hide-
> Hide in thy caves from shrapnel's deadly splash.

Yet 'mid thy ruins, shrine now desolate,
The Spring breaks thro' and visions many a spot
With promise of the wild–rose–tho' belate–
And the eternal blue forget–me–not.

So Nature flourishes amid decay,
Defiant of the fate that laid her low;
So Man in triumph scorning Death below
Visions the springtide of a purer day:

Dreams of the day when rampant there will rise
The flowers of Truth and Freedom from the blood
Of noble youth who died: when there will bud
The flower of Love from human sacrifice.

There by thr fallen youth, where heroes lie,
Close by each simple cross the flowers will spring,
The bonnes enfants will wander in Spring,
And lovers dream those dreams that never die.'

The period of rest and recuperation was not to last for long. With his poems bound and sent to the publisher, Will Streets once again allowed himself to be swallowed up by the unstoppable war effort. A date had been set for the assault, and there would be no turning back from hereon in. The designated night of 30 June 1916 approached quickly, and as the sun set and darkness fell, the battalion silently made their way to the assembly trenches which had been previously prepared to the rear of John Copse.

The trenches themselves had been victim to the relentless rainy weather, and were in a state of terrible disrepair when the battalion arrived. Their last haven of safety and shelter was nothing more than a collection of mudslides and caved–in dugouts. As such, the last hours before the Sheffield Pals threw their safety to the wind, and offered their lives for the plight of their nation, were spent face–down in mud, soaked to the skin by the waterlogged ground. Many of the soldiers reportedly joked that this was as bad as things could get; however, this sadly proved to be incorrect.

After a night of sheer discomfort, it was time for the big push. At 7:20am, 1 July, the first wave of the assault was signalled, and A and C companies began silently to crawl towards enemy lines, protected by only the barrage of artillery fire which flew over their heads, and exploded into the German front line which was rapidly becoming closer. At 7:29am, the second wave of the assault began to crawl into position, around 30 yards behind their advanced colleagues. The second wave included Sergeant John William Streets, who reportedly spent the final few moments before the assault silently ensuring that all the men in his charge were present, before waiting for the signal to attack.

Zero Hour arrived just a moment later, and on the sound of Streets' whistle, his men, along with every other soldier on the battlefield, sprang into action, rising from the mud and running, rifles raised, towards the enemy. It was just a matter of seconds before the attack had been identified by the German outposts, and as such, the attack party had managed to advance just a meagre few feet before the machine guns and artillery opened fire upon the descending British soldiers. This moment was captured in detail in the battalion War Diary;

'They were immediately met with very heavy machine gun and rifle fire and artillery barrage. The left half of 'C' Coy was wiped out before getting near the German wire, and on the right the few men who reached the wire were unable to get through. As soon as our barrage lifted from their front line, the Germans, who had been sheltering in their Dug-outs immediately came out and opened rapid fire with their machine guns.'

Those who managed to reach the German frontline immediately noticed that there had been an error; the barbed wire and trench system which had seemingly been under a barrage of artillery fire for the last week, was almost intact. There had been a miscalculation during the meticulous preparations. This left a small attack party of British troops facing one of the main German battle posts without assistance. As such, British casualties were becoming increasingly heavy. Hundreds were killed or wounded during these first few moments, amongst them was Streets, who had been seriously wounded by machine gun fire, and crawled, face down in the mud back to the British line.

However, before receiving treatment, Streets reportedly went back into the battle field to provide assistance in bringing back another, more seriously injured, soldier. This would be the last sighting of John William Streets. The attack had fallen into disarray, and the War Diary states that many of the wounded men had no choice to shelter in bomb craters until darkness fell. The next day, two patrols were sent out into No Man's Land to assess the situation, and just a few seriously wounded soldiers were brought back to the British lines. No ground had been gained, and the casualty reports recorded that 15 officers, and 468 soldiers were killed, wounded, or missing. Will Streets was listed amongst the missing; his plight being eerily similar to that of the hero in his poem 'The Wayside Cross'.

> 'The moon did wane, dawn stole above the hill,
> The lark in heaven poured forth his ecstasy;
> The orchard bloom'd, the winds were hushed and still
> And there amid the moon's serenity
> Firm-lipp'd and proud with victory on his face
> A soldier lay, 'he died for love of race.'

The Streets family had been given the cruellest news of all. Their beloved Will was reported as Missing in Action. For many, this was seen as a more terrible blow than news of the death of a loved one. The relatives of the deceased could mourn and seek solace in the noble death of their son, father or brother. For the Streets family, this was not to be. Any chance of survival for Will was miniscule, yet, without formal notification of his death, Sergeant Streets was nothing more than a ghost; a life which now straddled the realms of the living and the dead.

It was not until 1 May 1917 that the Streets family were to receive news of any kind. Sadly, it was the inevitable news that Will had been officially Killed in Action. An advanced patrol, plotting another assault on this infamous part of the Somme had discovered a number of bodies. Amongst them, identified by his regimental number, was Sgt John William Streets, who had lain for ten months beneath the battered and splintered trees of John Copse, surrounded by the earthly remains of several of his comrades.

Spurred on by the tragic demise of such a gifted poet, the publisher, Galloway Kyle, was moved to publish a posthumous collection of Will's poems entitled 'The Undying Splendour'. This featured a number of Streets' most evocative work, and contained verse written in the training camps of England, and on the battlefields of Egypt and the Somme. Will Streets would thankfully be given a final resting place, and his work would live on beyond his tender years, making his poem 'A Soldiers Cemetery' all the more poignant:

'Behind that long and lonely trenchèd line
To which men come and go, where brave men die,
There is a yet unmarked and unknown shrine,
A broken plot, a soldiers' cemet'ry.

There lie the flower of Youth, the men who scorned
To live (so died) when languished liberty:
Across their graves, flowerless and unadorned,
Still scream the shells of each artillery.

When war shall cease this lonely, unknown spot
Of many a pilgrimage will be the end,
And flowers will bloom in this now barren plot
And fame upon it through the years descend–
But many a heart upon each simple cross
Will hang the grief, the memory of its loss.'

The body of John William Streets was buried at Euston Road Cemetery, Colincamps. Although the exact location of his remains within the cemetery are unknown, due to the removal of the temporary markers which were replaced by the permanent war graves, an inscription, provided by the Streets family, at the foot of his official headstone reads:

I FELL: BUT YIELDED NOT
MY ENGLISH SOUL
THAT LIVES OUT HERE
BENEATH THE BATTLE'S ROLL

The following year, the guns fell silent. The war had ended, with the British and their allies the victors. The nation collectively celebrated the victory, and perhaps more enthusiastically, the end of the conflict which had taken the lives of at least one member of the majority of families. Street parties and parades were hastily organised in honour of the victorious army, yet it would be months before many of the soldiers would be demobbed; therefore, many of these celebrations would take place in the absence of the men who risked life and limb for this jubilant nation.

Confetti had turned into mulch clinging to the gutters by the time most of the soldiers had come home and the jubilation of victory had now become a quiet echo in the streets of a nation which had now returned to business as usual, but with its coffers empty and its resources dwindling. By the time the troop trains pulled into stations across the country, the fanfare was over, and the damaged men of war quietly and anonymously returned to their homes, back to the lives which had been placed on hold for the duration of the hostilities. Yet, the lives of these men were rarely a continuation of their previous existences. Thousands of businesses had closed down, meaning that a large percentage of the returning soldiers found themselves unemployed and penniless upon their humdrum return to society. Having waited for years for their fathers and husbands to return, families found themselves just as destitute as they had been in the absence of their loved ones.

The working class, of whom most of the victorious army was made up, quickly found housing to be unaffordable and employment almost impossible to find. Yet, the government still patted itself on the back and prided itself on a great and historic victory against imperialistic powers. The returning heroes, used as cannon fodder and transported back home like cattle, had been forsaken. Every promise of a new and improved society, which formed part of the propaganda to convince these men to fight in the first place, had been shamefully broken. There was no money for the war veterans, and very little in the way of future prospects.

For countless thousands, the hardships of life back home were also exacerbated by physical and psychological damage caused by the horrors of war. Those who had lost limbs or senses during the war now found themselves to be unemployable, reliant only on pitifully meagre payouts by the local authorities. The shell-shocked soldiers who suffered from what is now recognised as Post-Traumatic Stress Syndrome were institutionalised or left to the care of their families, never to receive any meaningful treatment. The worst of the hardship was borne by those who lived in the larger towns and cities; lost men fighting for the mere existence of the families amongst a sea of thousands who faced the same plight. Their neighbourhoods, once homely and industrious, became slums due to a lack of council investment and the sky-high levels of unemployment. More businesses were forced to close due to the lack of any paying customers, meaning more unemployment, leaving little or no chance for these inner-city areas ever to return to their former glories. For the majority of the population, their proudly victorious nation had become nothing but a black hole of poverty and despair.

As history so often teaches us, poverty and hopelessness are the catalysts to a rise in crime, and the working classes of Britain quickly found this to be the case. With no other means of feeding their families, and a sizeable sense of anger at the nation which had betrayed them, the men who once risked everything on the fields of Europe had no choice but to risk everything again; this time, in allowing themselves to be swallowed up by the evils of necessity. In every major city, criminal gangs began to take over the filthy streets and crumbling warehouses. Theft, gang warfare and illegal gambling became part of every working-class society. If the government would not provide for the returning soldiers, then they would take matters into their own hands. Families had to be fed, and money had to be made at any cost. Within a year, cities such as London, Manchester, Birmingham and Sheffield had all experienced a rise in crime, and very few residents were not aware of at least one criminal gang which plied its trade on their very doorsteps.

At the heart of Sheffield's descent into darkness was a man who had also served his country, albeit for a short time. He was a troublemaker and a deserter, who would carve his name into the history of the Steel City. His name was George Mooney, and for a considerable amount of time, he held the city of Sheffield in his palm.

Introduction

The Historic Gangs of Sheffield

'In a war, whichever side may call itself the victor, there are no winners,
but all are losers.'

Neville Chamberlain,
British Politician (1869–1940)

A s a major industrial city, Sheffield has always been a place where
the mood of the nation is reflected in its residents. Very little takes
place in London which does not spread north to the metropolises
of Sheffield, Manchester, Leeds and other large cities. Unfortunately, this
trend also includes the spread of negative events and behaviours. Therefore,
it is little wonder that the growth of gang culture which grew from the slums
of London due to the ever-decreasing quality of life experienced by its
inhabitants, would eventually travel north; such were the plummeting living
conditions and rocketing populations of the vast northern industrial centres.

It has always been the case that disaffected youths find meaning in
challenging authority, but in most cases, this is nothing more than a rite
of passage before embarking on a well spent life. Yet, it would seem that
when times are particularly hard, the transition between angry youth and
contented adult is a much wider gulf than would normally be the case. People
have always fought for several things, the wellbeing of their families, a sense
of worth, and the respect of others amongst other factors. The residents
of Sheffield have always been a spirited bunch, but the socially aware and
politically savvy activists of the modern city bear little resemblance to those
who preceded them.

The causes may be the same, but the means of protest have, thankfully,
evolved into peaceful and reasoned debate in most cases. We may not be
perfect in the north, but we're a damn sight more reasonable than our
forefathers it would seem, as the history of the city is awash with tales of gang
violence and organised crime. We protest now as it is our right to challenge
authority; our civil disobedience is nothing more than a chance to express

our opinions. Yet, in times gone by, civil disobedience was undertaken for very different reasons, as the ghosts of the past were victim to a society in which they were largely invisible, and any chance of gain was there for the taking.

The first real gang to make an impact upon the ordinary lives of the northern working class was the Northern Mob, which originated in the 1840s, and was made up of several local groups from as far away as Liverpool, Manchester, Derby and Nottingham. The mob included a large representation from Sheffield, as one would expect from such a growing industrial city. As is the case in so many gang tales, the main driving force behind the Northern Mob was financial gain.

The mob would mobilise at almost any event that could guarantee a high turnout of wealthy visitors. Agricultural shows, race meetings, boxing matches and animal baiting events were always targeted, as the chance to extort money by means of deception or sheer intimidation were always rife on these occasions. There were very few times when a wealthy Londoner would not part with his money when being surrounded by a large and unruly gang of northern thugs.

However, as time passed and the cities grew even further, the co-operative approach of the Northern Mob seems to have fallen by the wayside. There were now wealthy aspects of every city, and it no longer became necessary to join forces against the *Champagne Charlies* of the south. As such, the local factions began to concentrate on taking whatever they could from their hometowns. As in London, industry and invention had spread, but the proceeds of this were unjustly distributed. The working man was still on a pittance, while his employer or Member of Parliament was publicly rolling in clover.

By the time the 1860s arrived, Sheffield was no longer providing men to extort and intimidate in the name of the north. The city itself was beginning to find itself under the threat of its own local gangs, who worked their own particular neighbourhoods, offering protection in return for extortionate fees, and making the lives of those who refused to pay a misery.

The first two major gangs in Sheffield had very different rationales when choosing their prey. One chose to stalk the streets of the slums, keen to control their fellow working-class residents, and controlling the local businesses with violence and intimidation, whilst the other set their sights higher, and spent their days targeting the wealthier residents of the city.

The Guttapercha Gang was named after a resin used in some manufacturing processes. It was a gum which could be coated upon an object in order for it to solidify and create a rock hard coating; just the thing needed to cover a short piece of wood in order to create an effective cosh! This particular gang would patrol the slums of the workers, demanding protection money from the shops and pubs in the area. Such was their number, that the fledgling police reportedly refused to attend in situations where the gang were suspected to be involved, leaving the poor of the city to live in fear and misery.

One notable former member of the gang was infamous killer Charlie Peace, who took something of an honorary role amongst the younger men, using his reputation and criminal cunning to act as a kind of Fagin figure to the inexperienced thugs. It is also believed that Peace was the man who introduced the gang to the resin that spawned their unusual name, as he had often used this to create false appendages with which to hide his damaged and deformed hand.

In terms of prestige and honour, the Guttapercha Gang were very much at the bottom of the heap in this corner of South Yorkshire. Their practices of robbing from the poor were looked down on by every other criminal element of the city, and it was not long before the residents of the slums decided that enough was enough, and organised themselves in opposition to the gang. With their reign of fear over the slums quickly disappearing, and the rest of the city under the control of either the police or rival gangs, the death knell was rapidly approaching for the Guttapercha Gang, whose members would eventually slink back to their everyday lives, ridiculed and humiliated by those who had once been held in the shadow of a hastily manufactured cosh.

The other main gang in operation at the time was led by a well-known character who went by the name of Kingy Broadhead. Their main stomping ground was the lower end of the Park district, where the new train station was situated, and several upmarket establishments began to crop up to cater for the travelling gentry. Much of their ethos was to be a constant thorn in the side of the police who were tasked with protecting the wealthier inhabitants of the city, and it is a well-known and comical fact that nothing made the gang happier than one of their number knocking the top hat from a gentleman with a well-aimed stone! Yet, the gang did have a darker side, and while the majority of the miscreants were causing chaos outside the station, others would stalk the platforms, demanding money with menaces whilst the police dealt with the childish acts of their colleagues. This was a well thought out and successful ploy, which kept Kingy Broadhead and his men active for over a decade before the gang disbanded due to dwindling numbers.

Later came the gangs of the east end, who held this side of the city in their hands during the post First World War years. The first such gang to emerge was the Neepsend Gas Tank Gang, which thrived in the dimly lit and often unprotected streets of Neepsend and Shalesmoor, which was the natural route home for many of the city's industrial workers. Their methods were crude, and amounted to nothing more than robbing the returning steelworkers and miners at knifepoint. One cannot doubt that some serious money was made in this way, but their tenure as the resident east end gang was soon ended by the emergence of two much more organised and motivated groups.

The Red Silk and White Silk Gangs had once been one and the same, but had split due to some quarrel between themselves. Both operated in the east end of the city, and before their split, had been the gang that ousted the Gas Tank boys from the area. Having separated into two factions, the residents of the area were relieved to find that it would not be long before the main aim of the rival gangs was to attack each other, leaving the people of Neepsend and Shalesmoor largely unmolested! Both gangs favoured the Blonk Street fairground as their preferred territory, making their money by offering protection to the fairground workers, and picking the pockets of anyone who was unlucky enough to find themselves penned in by a crowd. However, the two former halves of the gang did have a common enemy, and when they found themselves face to face with their foe, sparks were bound to fly. The Reds and the Whites both loved a scrap with the army, and would happily join forces should they spot a number of squaddies attending the fair. This resulted in some shocking skirmishes, with the unprepared soldiers often being outnumbered by the thugs who seemed to appear from nowhere to attack them as they wandered through the fairground.

The last of the gangs to emerge worked out of the West Bar area, and were headed by a man of Irish descent whose name would be synonymous with gang culture in Sheffield; they were merely a gang of unskilled pickpockets and race track thugs at the time, but by the time the war had come and gone, there would be very few people in the city who would not have heard of the Mooney Gang.

The onset of the First World War brought with it the dissolution of the gangs, as most of the young men were of military service age, and chose to join up with their friends, rather than wait for their eventual and inevitable conscription. If nothing else, the army was offering them a wage and three meals a day. The battle for control of the city would have to wait; but by the time peace returned, there was only one gang that would reassemble.

Chapter 1

Mooney and the Sky-Ring

'The gambling known as business looks with austere disfavour upon the
business known as gambling.'

Ambrose Bierce – American Author (1842–1914)

In a city which lost over 6,000 men to the cruelty of the First World War,
men like George Mooney would ordinarily be shunned by their former
comrades. Clandestine glances and hushed insults would follow them
around their daily life, and any ounce of respect which had ever been earned
would quickly be cast into the wind. Sheffield was a city of the honourable
dead, and the heroic survivors. There was no place for a deserter in the Steel
City.

Yet, over a relatively short period of time, Mooney would not only recover
the respect he had lost due to his lack of military service; he would thrive on
the political and financial difficulties which loomed over the country like a
hangover of epic proportions. Like a rat feeding on the corpses of the fallen
soldiers, Mooney did what he had to in order to survive, but soon became
more than aware that an abundance of flesh lay beyond the safety of the
trenches, unprotected, and free to those who had the nerve to take it.

From his 'business' premises, high above the smoky industrial city,
Mooney saw before him a great vision of opportunity. The dot-like figures,
shuffling through the streets in search of work, would never be more pliable
than they were in the wake of a financially crippling war. They were lost;
without a leader, and without hope. Mooney would give them a chance,
albeit a small chance, to provide for their families and regain the lives they
could no longer afford to live. But, for every winner, there would be 100
losers, lining the pockets of the deserter and his cohorts.

George Mooney was of Irish descent, his forefathers having relocated
to South Yorkshire during the boom in industry, which promised work for
any man who left their hometown and allowed themselves to be swallowed
up by the ever-present smoky orange glow which perpetually hovered above

the city. The family had come to seek their fortune by means of honest toil, but their eventual offspring would find his own way in life, by any means possible.

By the age of 33, and having found that finding honest work was becoming more and more challenging with each passing day, Mooney had come to realise that his greatest assets were also the major flaws in his character. This was a man who was already branded as a deserter, and regarded as an untrustworthy thug; exactly the kind of man who no longer cared to rescue his reputation on the streets of his hometown.

Even as a teenager, before his infamous dalliance with the military, Mooney was regarded by most as a violent and volatile troublemaker. He would constantly find himself being dragged home to his exasperated father by the local police, having been caught fighting with other boys, or relieving people of their possessions. Unlike many youngsters who studied the art of pick-pocketing, Mooney would never prove to be very good at this covert method of theft; therefore, as he grew more and more physically intimidating, he learned that he could use his size and bravado to take whatever he wanted with nothing more than a threat.

Despite his notorious reputation, and the number of petty crimes for which he was arrested, Mooney was fortunate enough never to find himself on the receiving end of any serious punishment. He was no stranger to a night in the cells, but had yet to find himself being locked away for any serious amount of time. Yet, as he matured into a young man, his thirst for intimidation and violence grew along with his powerful frame, and one can imagine that it was almost a relief to his parents, by now modest publicans of a backstreet pub, when their son informed them that he was going to war.

Like John William Streets, Mooney found himself being enlisted into the Sheffield Pals Battalion, and seemed to thrive on the hardships of his basic training. The physical rigour and emotional turmoil of being turned into a soldier did not seem to affect him; he had come from a city where he was routinely avoided due to his violent and intimidatory tendencies, only to be thrust into a world where these negative character traits would be useful, and even rewarded.

Having found himself in the position where he was now being paid to hone his fighting skills, and learn new ones along the way, Mooney breezed through his basic training without breaking sweat. His short life thus far had been a prelude to finding an existence where his tough and resilient nature would flourish, and as such, he was lauded as a natural soldier, and an enlisted man with a bright military future ahead of him. However, as the training camps and gruelling drills faded into memory, and the real world of industrial war emerged, the bravado and courage of George Mooney also seems to have slipped into the past.

The last stop for the Pals Brigade in 1916, before arriving in war torn France, was an army base at Clipstone, Nottinghamshire. This was where the regiment was to finish its training, and the young volunteers were expected to be lean, steely eyed fighting men upon waving goodbye to this last safe haven. One would have expected George Mooney to be in his element in a training camp, the reputation of which had frightened many of his comrades before they even arrived at the gates. However, something about George Mooney had changed. His physical prowess and ability to lead others had earned him a promotion to the rank of corporal shortly before leaving for Nottinghamshire, yet, since this promotion, Mooney had become noticeably more withdrawn and thoughtful, choosing to spend his free time alone. He confided in a few close comrades that he was bored by army life, but this had never been an issue for Mooney before; indeed, he had thrived on the regimented lifestyle and physically tortuous regime.

Then, one evening, with no word to anyone, Mooney simply climbed the wire fencing of the camp and disappeared. It was the morning roll call before anybody realised he had gone missing; such was the quiet and solitary demeanour of the corporal in the days before this unexplained occurrence. It was a matter of mere days before the Military Police caught up with Mooney, who had arrived back in Sheffield, telling those who recognised him that he was on leave, and spending his brief sabbatical in a drunken stupor which took him from pub to pub across the length of the city.

It was only Mooney's previous promotion, and his reputation as a promising soldier which saved him from a spell in Military Prison, which during the First World War, was designed to be as brutal as possible, acting as a deterrent for those who, like Mooney, had decided that the army life was not for them. Instead, he was returned to Clipstone, where he was summarily relieved of his new rank, and placed into a cell for a number of days as a warning that this kind of behaviour would not be tolerated, even from a soldier as impressive as the newly demoted Private Mooney. Taking his punishment quietly, and without making a fuss, Mooney spent his short confinement brooding in silence. To all intents and purposes, this appeared to be the case of a wild stallion that just needed one more gallop in the fields and had now been broken into submission. Again, without any kind of fuss, Mooney was released back into his regiment, where he would again do everything that was asked of him, but remain in his withdrawn and thoughtful state.

If the military authorities thought that they had managed to beat Mooney into a state of quiet compliance, they were entirely incorrect, as, at the first opportunity he found, Mooney once again scaled the fences and left the camp without a word to anyone. It would appear that he had learned from his previous jaunt, and this time, did not underestimate the dogged persistence of the Military Police. Private Mooney would not be returning to the army, and would not be fighting the enemy alongside his local pals.

For the next two years, the whereabouts of George Mooney are something of a mystery. He was a wanted man in Sheffield, and would have been arrested on sight had he been foolish enough to return to his hometown. The common consensus was that he had somehow managed to escape to Ireland, where he was harboured by his extended family until the end of the war. This does seem entirely plausible, as no member of the Military Police would have been foolish enough to set foot in Ireland at the time; such was the political climate between Dublin and Whitehall after the Easter Rising of 1916, in which blood was shed on both sides as the Irish Republican Brotherhood made their bid for independence.

By the end of the war, the military simply did not have the resources or the inclination to round up the deserters who began to resurface, and, before the ink was even dry on the Armistice agreement, Mooney had sauntered brazenly back into Sheffield. His return was aided by a catalogue of lies, which varied depending on which old friend he was talking to. To some, he had been transferred to an elite regiment; to others, he had been invalided due to being wounded whilst undertaking some heroic action against the enemy.

However, the lies had very little in the way of substance, and it was not long before the holes in Mooney's account of things soon began to widen, until the whole façade became transparent enough for others to challenge his feeble tales of fictional heroism. George Mooney was one of the few individuals to return home in 1918 with a diminished reputation, and it was this loss of a formerly fearsome reputation that would gradually turn the deserter into a General. Nobody feared George Mooney any more, and nobody would give the time of day to such a cowardly deserter. But, this was a man who thrived on reputation and intimidation. As such, there was only one way to win back his notoriety; to win the hearts and minds of his fellow Sheffielders, and allow them to be in his debt, until he held enough souls in the palm of his hand to challenge for real power.

The 'Tossing Ring' at Sky Edge had been in existence since before the war, a deserted building which was frequently visited by a few addicted gamblers, who would turn up each day to try to win back the money which they had lost the day before. Business wasn't particularly good, and it was without much effort that George Mooney managed to attach himself to the management of the business, before eventually making it into his own grubby and immoral empire. The location of the 'Sky Ring' was one of the main reasons that it was one of the few illegal gambling dens to have survived the war. The few working men, who occupied skilled positions within the steel and coal industries, and had remained in the city during the conflict had more often than not chosen to take their business up the steep hill to Sky Edge, given that it was the establishment which was the least likely to be raided by the police. Due to this, where other venues went out of business, the Sky Ring managed to survive the war financially, albeit by the skin of its teeth.

The Ring had been established by a track bookmaker by the name of 'Snaps' Jackson, who was the wayward offspring of one of Sheffield's premier racing families. Always keen to make a few extra shillings, Jackson quickly identified that money could be made from the masses even on non-racing days, and as such, brought the simple practice of coin tossing to Sheffield; carefully selecting the derelict Sky Edge building as the perfect clandestine gambling den. Gambling was an illegal activity at the time, and was dealt with by the police as seriously as any other criminal offence.

Before long, he had established a growing clientele, largely made up of the steelworkers and coal miners of the city. It wasn't all sooty and bedraggled labourers however, as it was common knowledge that local hero, and Sheffield United and England goalkeeper Bill 'Fatty' Foulkes was also a regular at the Ring, occasionally supplementing his wage with a few winning wagers, but mostly handing his cash over to Jackson on a daily basis. As the business flourished, the word spread of the opportunity to make some extra money, and it was just a matter of weeks from the creation of the Sky Ring, that it was being frequented by gamblers from across the county, travelling by bus, train and tram from Rotherham, Barnsley, Doncaster and Chesterfield; most of them would leave the Ring with nothing more than their fare home and an excuse ready for their wives.

The first wagers would generally be placed at around 10:30am each day, and the action would continue until late in the night. It was only when Jackson decided to call it a day that his employees would be relieved of their various duties and the run-down building locked up securely for the night. There were no days when the Ring did not ply its trade; even on racing days,

Jackson would happily leave the running of the Ring to one of his faithful deputies. The Ring employed a number of local men. Those closest to Jackson were entrusted with dealing with the money, and others employed as 'flippers', who would be responsible for tossing three coins into the air, with the money being made or lost on which side the coins landed. There were also the 'pikers', who were usually local youths, who were charged with the task of manning strategically planned lookout points, and sending even younger runners to the Ring should the police be spotted on the steep ascents to the Sky Ring.

It was only the onset of war which stopped the growth of this tawdry empire. 'Snaps' Jackson was conscripted in 1916, and was forced to leave the running of the business to his brothers, who also found themselves on the King's Shilling before too long. It was during this period of transition that an event took place which was to damage and devalue the reputation of this once booming business and which saw the Sky Ring leaving the hands of the Jacksons for the first time since its creation. As the war raged across the Channel, the Ring had become something of a haven for deserters and conscription dodgers. This meant that a new enemy had become involved in the war against illegal gambling. Whilst the local police often turned a blind eye to the goings-on at the top of the hill (many of the constables are rumoured to have been regulars at the Ring themselves), the Military Police were guilty of no such apathy, and would stop at nothing to ensure that these traitors and cowards were delivered as quickly as possible back into the hands of the army.

The military operation to infiltrate the Sky Ring spared no expense or effort, and on one fateful morning in late 1916, the iron clad defence of the Ring was breached in spectacular style. The first sign of trouble came when spotters reported a bi-plane buzzing over the venue, seemingly circling the area. With the Ring almost at capacity, and a huge amount of money at stake, the Jackson brothers made the unwise decision to carry on, severely underestimating the might of the enemy that was about to come their way. What followed was a co-ordinated attack. One by one the pikers sent their runners to report approaching soldiers, and before the assembled gamblers could make their escape, a combined army of Military Police and mounted local police were rapidly approaching the Ring by every possible route. The place was quickly surrounded, and with the gamblers doing their best to barricade the doors, the final coup de grace was launched.

Residents of nearby Duke Street would later inform the press that they had observed an unmarked bus chug its way up the hill shortly after the building had been surrounded, and from this inconspicuous vehicle poured an entire company of armed soldiers. The invaders immediately lined up outside the Sky Ring, and the order was given to fix bayonets. Reportedly, the onrushing soldiers had barely even reached the doors of the building, before the barricades were taken down, and the first flurry of gamblers began to emerge into the daylight, their hands raised above their heads.

Over 100 men were arrested during this operation, including the Jackson brothers, who now bore the unwanted reputation as being the men who finally allowed the security of the Sky Ring to be breached. The deserters and draft dodgers were taken away without delay, and those who had simply fancied a few bets on this fateful morning were taken to appear before the magistrates on charges of illegal gambling. All in all, it was expected that this surprise attack would be the end of the Sky Ring.

However, with the Jackson brothers being taken into custody (from where they would be quickly conscripted and sent overseas), another local man, who was a well respected acquaintance of the Jackson family decided that all was not lost, and local bookmaker William Cowan quietly slipped into the shabby office of the Sky Ring. There was to be no grand reopening or triumphant fanfare, as Cowan was a wiser man than those he had replaced. He simply allowed business to trickle slowly back to Sky Edge, doubling the number of pikers employed by the Ring, and being satisfied with a more meagre income.

In this manner, the Sky Ring survived the war, understated and covertly guarded. However, the income and reputation of the place had become a mere shadow of its former self. Only the most hardened gamblers now risked the steep climb to the dilapidated building, and Cowan freely admitting that he would have no qualms in walking away from his business, should anyone else be foolish enough to pay the modest sum needed to take it off his hands.

One of the few regular visitors to the punch drunk shadow of the Sky Ring was a man who needed no introduction to his fellow gamblers. Once a fearsome street bully, but now a brooding and quiet deserter, George Mooney had been back in town for a number of weeks; his reputation in tatters, and seemingly friendless and without direction. Yet, his regular visits to the Ring were more than met the eye. He would make the odd bet and chat to the odd wary punter, but Mooney was making his daily trips to the Ring for a very different reason. Despite his many failings, one could never say that George Mooney was not astute. He had spent his early manhood heading his own fledgling gang of thugs, and had been able to escape a number of lengthy prison sentences due to his ability to cry poverty and remorse whilst being hauled before the magistrates. The few short sentences he had served had done nothing more than toughen the resolve of this determined character, and give him the opportunity to learn from the older, more experienced convicts.

His previous convictions ranged from street robbery to illegal bookmaking. He was a young man who was just as capable of robbing a passer-by at knifepoint, as he was setting up an unlicensed trading post at some of the less salubrious racing meetings. This was a man driven by a desperate desire for money and power, and before his disgrace in deserting his country, he looked every inch the blossoming gangster, right down to the sharp suits and concealed blade.

Without his fearsome reputation to rely on, Mooney began to collect a small band of followers made up other social misfits. He lent small amounts of cash to the gambling addicts at the Ring, bought drinks for the alcoholics in the local pubs, and on more than one occasion, provided a false alibi for acquaintances who had fallen foul of the law. To piece together a resurgent Mooney Gang, the Ringleader required all of his erstwhile followers to be in his debt. He did not yet require men he could trust, but men he could control.

Having ingratiated himself with William Cowan, Mooney soon convinced the bookmaker that he had all the nous and guile required to be a valuable asset to the Sky Ring. Asking only a small wage, Mooney took the role of 'headman', co-ordinating the pikers and runners, and ensuring that not a penny of the Ring's money went astray. Whilst his new role did nothing to increase the turnover of the Sky Ring, Mooney had at least shown that he was more than capable of its everyday running, and when the new headman had saved enough money to make a serious offer to William Cowan, the bookmaker had no hesitation in handing over the keys to the Sky Ring.

Whether by luck or by design, Mooney had picked the perfect time to procure the gambling den. His takeover coincided with the return of thousands of soldiers, all with war wages in their pockets, but no employment to keep them busy. The influx of ready money would not last for long, but Mooney was ready to take every penny he could, and welcomed his new customers with open arms. He was offering them the chance to increase their meagre stipends many times over, an offer which was difficult to refuse for those who had no means of regular income.

In addition to the returning soldiers, there were the local coalminers, who had been awarded a payout of 'Sankey' money, an amount paid to a percentage of miners for their loyal service in remaining at the coalface and providing the nation's fuel during the war. Again, this was money which Mooney could skilfully divert into his own pocket. The opportunity would not last for long, and he had to work quickly to ensure that as many people as possible passed through the doors of his new empire.

Using his ragtag band of followers, Mooney employed a number of methods to attract people to the Ring. He would often send one of his followers out to local pubs with a pocketful of cash, and instruct them to boast that they had tripled their money on one round of coin tossing. Of course, the money was to be returned to the business immediately, save for a few pennies spent on ale. Other promotional tactics included selling ale after the pubs had closed (an apparent godsend for the alcoholics of the city) and allowing his clients to gamble not only with money, but with possessions which would be summarily (and inaccurately) valued by one of his employees, before being rapidly exchanged for a handful of coins, which would immediately be placed on the next round of betting. Rather than working on restoring his reputation, Mooney had simply bought back respect and infamy. His gang of followers increased day by day, and, although he rarely trusted these men with anything more than the most basic tasks, the sheer number of men at his disposal had made Mooney a force to be reckoned with once more.

Within weeks of the resurgence of the Sky Ring, George Mooney was the talk of the town. Even his status as a deserter was beginning to fade, as it was drilled into his followers that Mooney had not deserted, he had spent the war in military prison for attacking a senior officer. As false as this story was, it soon become widely accepted, such was the number of people who claim to have known this as a fact.

With the war a quickly diminishing memory, and enforced government spending cuts, the local police proved to be nothing but a minor thorn in Mooney's side. On the few occasions that the police decided to climb the hill to Sky Edge, they would find nothing more than an empty building, and a few suspiciously busy pubs in the area. Illegal gambling no longer seemed to be of much concern to the authorities. They were happy enough to turn a blind eye, as long as this largely harmless pastime did not develop into anything more serious.

With his reputation restored (albeit cosmetically), Mooney was soon on the lookout for more trustworthy companions. His gang of debtors had played their part admirably, and most of them would continue as foot soldiers under the command of the former corporal, but there were people within the city who Mooney had earmarked as future officers within his rapidly growing gang. These were faces from Mooney's past, and he would not rest until he had succeeded in bringing his old gang back together.

The old Mooney gang had been made up of youths from two main areas of the city, West Bar and the Park Area, which is now well known as the site for the iconic Park Hill Flats. From the West Bar neighbourhood were Mooney himself, 'Spud' Murphy, Peter Winsey and Tommy Rippon, all of whom had spent their teens getting up to no good with their friend, George. Mooney's younger brother, John, was also a fringe member of the fledgling gang, but seems to have kept his nose far cleaner than that of his domineering older brother. From the Park area were Sam Garvin, William Furniss, William Roberts and Sandy Bowler, who formed the wider group, along with George 'Ganner' Wheywell and Frank Kidnew, who lived in the city centre, which was something of a middle ground in the dynamic of the group. Although the young group were separated by their respective neighbourhoods, as a gang, they could not have been closer.

The gang started out in the same way that most gangs come to life; a group of disillusioned young men who find kindred souls in their battle against authority. Their beginnings were fairly typical, with the lads of the Mooney Gang competing against each other to see who could pick the most pockets whilst on their travels around the city. It is suggested however, that not many of the gang were particularly adept at making money with sleight of hand tactics, which would ultimately lead to an escalation into brute force.

The gang soon moved into 'bottling', which was basically the act of mugging, but in a violent, intimidatory and mob-handed way. When the gang surrounded an unfortunate victim, there was no possibility of them escaping unharmed unless they readily agreed to part with their money and possessions. Although the group seemed to have a natural talent for these brutal tactics, it would seem that their brazen approach was somewhat lackadaisical, as a few of the gang would receive short prison sentences for street robbery before they reached manhood. As the gang aged together, their methods of extortion began to evolve. They were well aware of the trouble they would find themselves in should they continue to employ these strong-arm tactics, and began to employ a little brain power to complement their obvious brawn. With no real influence within the gambling fraternity, the youngsters made their money by hopping onto the trains which serviced the race tracks and card-sharping the drunken punters as they made their way home. The violent tactics did rear their ugly head now and again, but only if the victim refused to pay what was owed, or made a song and dance about the rigged games.

It wasn't long before the gang became well known around the tracks, and their number swelled to the number of men required making themselves a physical threat against the more established illegal bookmakers. They were tacitly allowed a small table at the edge of the betting concourse, as long as they did not try to fleece customers from their older and more hardened rivals. Yet, as the Mooney Gang swelled in number, so did their ambition, and within a year of their arrival at the race tracks, the gang were routinely making threats to the established bookmakers, turning over tables and pocketing money in the process. This was a gang to be reckoned with, and only a major twist of fate could stop them in their tracks.

The twist of fate arrived in 1915, when the regular army had found themselves hopelessly outnumbered in the face of the enemy. Knowing that they would soon be conscripted into the army, and spread across any number of regiments, the gang made the wise choice to enlist, and at least have the opportunity to stay together. However, on joining the Sheffield Pals Battalion, most of the gang members still found themselves in separate companies from their friends. This was the end of the youthful Mooney Gang, and, had there been no war to concentrate on, the people of central Sheffield would breathe a collective sigh of relief. The boys were sent overseas to become men, all but their brave leader, George Mooney, who would have to wait a considerable amount of time before regaining enough influence to reunite his former cohorts under his leadership.

It was not until Mooney had made the re-born Sky Ring a success that he was able to even entertain the idea of calling upon his former gang members, but with money in his pocket, and plenty of muscle to back him up, the former leader once again found himself worthy of paying a visit to the battle-hardened men he had left behind at Clipstone Camp. Mooney had no idea of the reception he would receive, but decided that the time was as good as any to call his former soldiers back into line.

Again, the social climate was on Mooney's side, as the majority of his former friends had arrived home from the war without gainful employment to fall back on, and it was possibly with more of a financial motive, than an honourable one, that the first few men called upon agreed to join Mooney in his gambling operation. They had been promised a wage, and with the first few catches in the bag, the rest were soon to follow. Having made the journey to Sky Edge, the returning soldiers went to work as Mooney's enforcers for nothing more than financial gain. Yet after being invited to stay behind for free ale and food on several occasions, it was not long before talk turned to the old days, and a friendship between Mooney and his new employees began to blossom again. This was everything that Mooney had hoped for, and set the ball in motion for the development of his wider plans.

The Sky Ring continued to succeed, and for the next couple of years, the reputation of Mooney and his gang once again began to spread across the city. The Sky Ring was a place where it was possible to supplement a meagre income, but was also a place where one could literally lose the shirt from one's back. The enforcers had done their jobs so efficiently that they had almost done themselves out of a job. Nobody would dare to renege on a bet at the Sky Ring; to do so would mean extreme danger for themselves and their families.

With the business in Sky Edge now running itself on reputation alone, the reformed Mooney Gang found themselves discussing expansion back into the race tracks and protection rackets. However, the good times were soon to be a thing of the past, as the nation's finances, which had so often played into Mooney's hands, finally began to turn against him. His luck had held out for long enough, and like many of his customers, Mooney was about to experience a downturn in fortune.

The cowardly corporal would have to find it within himself to make some tough decisions, and the strength in unity of his gang would be tested to the limit. Now was a time for a strong and level-headed leader, and even Mooney himself would have wondered if he was strong enough to withstand the backlash that was about to come his way.

Chapter 2

Garvin's Army

'There are no absolute rules of conduct, either in peace or war.
Everything depends on circumstances.'

Leon Trotsky, Russian Revolutionary (1879–1940)

T he empire which had been carefully nurtured by George Mooney
had begun to crumble, and it was all because of a ridiculous decision
and carefully fudged set of figures created hundreds of miles away
in the heart of London. With the nation still bearing the cost of the war,
a report was created which suggested that the cost of living for ordinary
folk had actually dropped since before the war. Obviously, the author of the
report had not visited the slums which had sprung up in every major city.

As such, the nationalised industries were soon to be instructed to lower
wages accordingly, taking away any spare cash that the steelworkers or
miners had left over after providing for their families. There was anger at
this decision, of course, but the management of these industries could do
nothing but tow the party line, and follow the brutal instructions set out to
them by David Lloyd George's government.

In an industrial city such as Sheffield, this was a measure which would
affect the majority of households, who could now rely on a small amount
of benefits should they become unemployed, but would see their weekly
income drop in order to pay for these new privileges. There was simply no
money available for vices, and those who did still attend the gambling dens
were waging pennies instead of pounds.

The drop in income hit the Sky Ring hard, and although Mooney
managed to fare better than many of his rivals, he soon became only too
aware that his business would have to be stripped back in order for it still to
make a workable profit. This led to a decision which would spark an untold
amount of trouble on the streets of Sheffield for years to come, and would
severely impact on the gang that Mooney had assembled around him in
order to succeed.

The Sky Ring enforcers, made up of Mooney's closest allies, were on a very good wage. This had been a necessary evil in order to bring his old cohorts back into the fold. Yet, in times of true hardship, everybody becomes expendable. He could either follow the actions of the government, lowering the wages of his senior employees, thereby risking the loss of the support he had worked so hard to win back; or, he could attempt to keep some of them happy, whilst dispensing entirely of the services of others.

Mooney, after careful consideration, opted for the latter. His empire simply could not sustain this number of men on their highly inflated wages. As such, it was simply a decision of who to keep, and who to oust from his band of brothers. The answer to the puzzle was ultimately one of geography. He would keep the services of the West Bar men, as this was his neighbourhood, and he had known many of them since his early childhood, and would dispense of the services of the Park Hill men, who had also been loyal followers, but had entered the fray a little later than the others.

This meant the end of an era for William Furniss, William Roberts and Sandy Bowler, all of whom took the news badly, and tried in vain to convince the West Bar men to join them in the search for new ventures. However, in these days of austerity, a good wage was hard to come by, and it was with deep regret that the remaining members of the gang were forced to turn their backs on their former cohorts, and pledge allegiance to George Mooney, such was the influence he now held over their lives, and those of their young families. The hasty restructuring of the Sky Ring hierarchy now meant that Mooney would run the Ring alongside his older brother, John, and his most trusted friend, Peter Winsey. Winsey had been a part of Mooney's life seemingly forever, as he had been taken in by Mooney's parents after the death of his own mother, and was a third Mooney brother in all but name. The huge gambling operation had now been stripped back to being a family business.

The other West Bar men were kept on as enforcers, taking orders from The Mooneys and Winsey. As this had been the natural way of things during their younger gang days, Spud Murphy, Frank Kidnew and Albert Foster were more than happy to accept the change in hierarchy, and continued in their employment as readily as ever. Unfortunately, in doing so, the rift between Mooney and the Park Hill men now widened to include those who were seen as having sold their souls for a wage at the Sky Ring.

The ousted men were seething, and it was not long before they revisited an old acquaintance. Sam Garvin had been one of the men originally handpicked by Mooney in the formation of his elite gang, but had since left the employment of his former gang leader, having never really been convinced of Mooney's intentions, or of the stories which had been fabricated in order to rescue the reputation of the thuggish deserter. Plans were quickly hatched to form a gang which would be able to rival Mooney's in terms of brute force and criminal cunning. None of these men had ever shied away from an altercation, and would certainly not allow themselves to be humiliated by men like of Mooney. The talk was of revenge and violence, a chance to get even with those who had forsaken them in favour of a few shillings from the hand of a deserter.

Yet, under the guiding influence of the intelligent and ambitious Garvin, a new aim was established. The Sky Ring was situated in *their* neighbourhood, and as such, should be in the hands of those who hailed from the streets overlooking the city. With this new goal to aim for, and a fresh sense of injustice in their hearts, this group of cast-offs turned their minds to reclaiming what they believed to be rightfully theirs, and thus, the Park Brigade was born.

The first job for the Park Brigade was to swell its numbers in order to rival that of the extended Mooney Gang, and for this particular job, Sam Garvin chose his closest friend and ally, Sandy Bowler. Bowler was an ex-prize fighter, and boasted a fearsome reputation amongst the regulars of the pubs in the Park Hill district. All that was required was to convince the men of the neighbourhood that a deserter from across the city held control of what was rightfully theirs.

With this in mind, Bowler, along with William Furniss and William Roberts, began to wander the streets of Park Hill on a nightly basis. They would stop in every pub and billiard hall, garnering support for their cause, and deliberately seeking out those who were reported to be in possession of a violent streak. There was no money to be offered, just a sense of righteousness and civic duty. The money would come when the Sky Ring was theirs. Before long, the Park Brigade had grown in number to almost double that of the extended Mooney Gang. Meetings were held in taprooms and snooker clubs, where the erudite Sam Garvin would step onto his soapbox and address those who had joined him in his crusade to overthrow George Mooney from his lofty position amidst their own neighbourhood. The men were chomping at the bit, and all that was left was to wait for the right opportunity.

Amongst those who were attendance during Garvin's rousing speeches were two brothers, Lawrence and Wilfred Fowler. At the younger end of the

Park Brigade demographic, the two possessed all the enthusiasm one would expect from men in their early twenties, but were eyed suspiciously as being naive and inexperienced by their new taskmasters. However, the two would play a huge part in the battle for control of the city in the subsequent years.

The takeover of the Sky Ring was something of an anticlimax given the rabble rousing and troop gathering which had taken place over the previous weeks, and certainly did not match the drama of the last time the Ring was infiltrated by the Military Police. It was a short war of attrition, intimidation, and carefully targeted attacks. Knowing full well that the Sky Ring was protected by lookouts posted on every street corner, and wholly aware that they would find themselves barricaded out of the building should a mob handed arrival be spotted, Garvin chose to wage his war wisely. Rather than oust Mooney by a large-scale show of force, he would simply make life in Park Hill impossible for the Mooney Gang, therefore taking his prize by default.

His first move was to make the Mooney Gang aware of the force they would have to reckon with, sending out huge groups of men to stand on the streets opposite the Ring in order to intimidate any approaching customers. Without the funds flowing in from the working men, the gambling den would be losing money within a matter of days. The second phase of the attack came as the number of visitors to the Ring began to dwindle. This time, the plan was to convince or intimidate the fringe gang members to switch allegiance. They were warned that there would soon be no money to pay them, and that they risked life and limb should they ignore the warning, and find themselves on the losing side of a turf war. Having successfully relieved Mooney of many of his gang members, the last course of action was to spell out the situation to Mooney himself, and allow him to leave the Sky Ring without bloodshed. Several notes were pushed under the heavily barricaded doors, in which Garvin offered the chance for the remaining Mooney Gang to quietly leave the area without threat or hindrance.

Although never formally responding to the warnings, Mooney did take heed of the situation, and was wise enough to see that his position was now untenable. He could risk everything and defend his empire, or he could retreat and plot his eventual revenge. Despite his many failings, George Mooney was wise enough to see that the second option was by far the better; he had taken the Ring once, and was convinced that he was capable of doing it again.

Without fanfare or fireworks, the battle was won. There was no pitched battle, or chaos in the streets. Mooney simply did not arrive at the Sky Ring one morning, nor did his employees. Within hours the vacated office was claimed by Sam Garvin, and word was spread that the Sky Ring was under new management.

No doubt seething in defeat, the Mooney Gang remained within the friendly streets of West Bar for a number of weeks. They simply did not have the numbers to form any kind of army capable of retaking the Sky Ring. Instead they returned to their families, meeting each day to discuss the situation, and pitching ideas across taproom tables as to how they would regain their empire. Mooney had taken note of Garvin's tactics employed against him, and quickly identified that a number of small battles were required to break the unity of the Park Brigade. He would tackle his tormentors one by one, until Garvin no longer had the service of the former Mooney Gang generals. The turncoats, no matter how valid their reason for joining Garvin, would be the first to receive their comeuppance.

In order to take his enemies by surprise, it was necessary for Mooney and his gang to keep a very low profile for a while. In fact, it was almost three months since losing control of the Sky Ring in January 1923, until any kind of retribution was launched. The aim was to spread fear across the upper echelons of the Park Brigade, and the planned opening attack was to be personal, brutal, and terrifying.

It was on the night of 29 April that two men, brandishing pokers and wearing scarves to disguise their features, arrived quietly in Duke Street Lane, a rundown street in the Park Hill area. As the street lay amidst a warren of slum housing, it was vital that the attack take place as quickly and quietly as possible, and working in silence, whilst keeping a constant lookout, it was a matter of minutes before the two masked men had found a window with a frame suitably rotted to allow them to work it open without the need for any unwanted noise. Having managed to slide the window up, and climbing into the house, taking care not to make a sound, the two intruders tiptoed up the rickety stairs. Their target was alone (it is not known whether he lived alone, or whether the attack had been deliberately co-ordinated in the absence of his family) and sleeping heavily in the larger of the two bedrooms. There was a brief moment of pause, as the pokers were held aloft, before they came crashing down on the slumbering body of former Mooney Gang member, William Furniss. Waking only briefly, before being beaten into unconsciousness, the man who had formerly been a miner at the nearby Nunnery Colliery until being tracked down by his former gang boss was given no chance to defend himself. The attack was brutal and swift, and within a minute of entering the room, the two masked men were making their way back down the stairs, and out of the window, before discarding the pokers and scarves, and splitting up to wander inconspicuously home.

By the next morning, Furniss had regained consciousness, and had no choice but to cry for help, such were the injuries inflicted upon him. A gaping head wound, several broken ribs and a broken arm were discovered on his eventual admittance into hospital. However, Furniss was unwilling or unable to describe his attackers to the police constable who was sent for. Yet, it would seem that he *was* certain who it was that had entered his home and committed such a violent assault. When, having gained some of his strength a few days later, Furniss was able to meet with Sam Garvin, he confided to his new employer that his attackers had been Frank Kidnew and Spud Murphy. These were men he had known and been friends with for many years, and even a scarf tied around the face was insufficient to disguise their identity, even during his brief period of consciousness on that fateful night. Needless to say, Garvin was furious about such a cowardly attack being launched against one of his top men, and immediately set about plotting a revenge attack against Mooney and his gang. However, the revenge attack would be anything but silent and calculated, it would be a show of force against his enemy, and would take place on their very own streets.

It was less than a month later, on 18 May, that a number of Park Brigade members wandered into Corporation Street, West Bar at 6am. Their spotters had informed them that several members of the Mooney Gang had been drinking all night, and had spent the last few hours in a house of 'ill repute'. This was the perfect moment to catch them off guard, and the moment the men set foot out of the house, they were greeted by a hail of flying bricks and bottles from the other side of the street. Having quickly run out of missiles, the assembled Park Brigade members ran across the street to engage their prey in hand to hand combat. It was a scene of pure chaos, as around twenty men, most of them from Park Hill, brawled viciously in the early morning streets. Being the location of a police station, it was not long before the residents of West Bar raised the alarm, and a group of constables ran towards the temporary battleground. Yet, it was this show of authority which broke up the brawl in the most ironic manner. The only people the gang members despised more than each other were the police, and as their approach was spotted, the bricks which had been launched at the Mooney Gang, were now picked up again and thrown in the direction of the oncoming constabulary. This was gang business, and it was an unspoken rule that the police had no business sticking their noses into the affairs of either faction. Several policemen and one passer-by were injured by the flying bricks, before the group of brawlers had split up and made their getaway in every direction. All but one of the men made it to safety, that is, apart from George Mooney's closest ally. Peter Winsey had been badly beaten, as the Mooney Gang had found themselves outnumbered by almost three to one. He had managed to hold off his attackers without being too seriously injured but the exertions of the morning had taken their toll and it was in a state of near exhaustion that he was quickly grabbed by an onrushing constable.

The injuries to the policemen and the elderly resident (named as Henry Onley, landlord of the nearby West Bar Hotel) must be answered for, and as only Winsey was taken down the road and thrown into a cell, he would be the man to stand before the magistrate in order to answer the charges, and shed some light on the cause of the affray.

Being an old hand in the gang lifestyle, there was no way on earth that Winsey was going to act as an informant against either side; he knew only too well that his life was in danger should he assist the police in any way. As such, he simply pleaded not guilty and refused to give any reason for the seemingly unprovoked attack to which he and his friends had fallen victim. He informed the magistrate that he had attended a ball at the Cutler's Hall in the City Centre, before walking to 'a certain house' with his friends. He would not name these friends, and was equally tight lipped when asked for the identity of his attackers. Yet, he was more than happy to shoulder the punishment meted out by the court, which amounted to a paltry £1 fine for the assault on Henry Onley, and £6 for an injury caused to a PC Sapsford.

In the public gallery was George Mooney, who sat in silence during the proceedings, before waiting at the prisoner's gate to greet his old friend and surrogate brother. The two briefly re-entered the court, where the fine was paid immediately and in full by Mooney, who described himself as Winsey's employer, although he failed to comment on exactly what business he was in.

The sense of injustice felt by the Mooney Gang was unquenchable. They had been the victims of the attack, and yet Peter Winsey had been the man to answer the charges, and George Mooney the man to end up out of pocket. Despite the sense of outrage, Mooney warned his charges to remain calm, and concentrate on finding another way to hit back at the enemy. The revenge attack for the brutal beating of William Furniss had been a warning that anything Mooney could do, Sam Garvin could retaliate to tenfold. Therefore, the next move had to be considered carefully, and would also need to be a powerful enough blow to make the eventual retaliation worth it. Several ideas were suggested, including the burning down of the Sky Ring, preferably with Garvin and his men still inside, joining forces with another gang from the region, or most chillingly, the public execution of Sam Garvin. Yet, none of these plans would come into fruition, as the period of contemplation was interrupted by an act of bravado and stupidity from one of Mooney's original gang.

Just over a week after the mass brawl on Corporation Street, Frank Kidnew, who was well known as a violent and impulsive thug, decided to take matters into his own hands, as he firmly believed that the war would not be won at the drawing board. Kidnew had been friends with Mooney and Winsey since childhood, and would not stand to see his fellow gang members belittled in such a way. Failing to inform the rest of the gang of his badly conceived plan, Kidnew left his home on the morning of 27 May and began to stride his way determinedly up the climb to Park Hill. His plan was to bide his time in hiding, and accost Sam Garvin the moment he appeared without the protection of his followers. It was a plan that lacked subtlety, and more importantly, lacked any planning at all. Being, as he had been, a key member of the Sky Ring security team, Kidnew should have been well aware that anyone approaching the area would have observed by pikers before they got within 100 yards of the building. Yet, with the red mist seriously limiting his vision, Kidnew seemed to have forgotten all about this, and had also forgotten that he would at the very least require some kind of disguise, being known, as he was, to all and sundry on top of the hill.

It was less than half an hour later that a man digging in his garden on Manor Laithe Road saw Kidnew for the second time. He had paid very little attention the first time to the man striding up the hill, but could not fail to notice him the second time. He was being dragged down the hill by three men, and looked as if he had spent the last half an hour rolling on the floor of an abattoir. Leaving Kidnew at the bottom of the hill, the three men quickly made the ascent to safety. Shortly after, two men came across Kidnew in his bloodied state, and found the man with a serious wound on his forehead, and his clothes shredded to pieces. In testament to the character of Frank Kidnew, despite his injuries he was grinning and smoking a cigarette as they arrived, jokingly saying 'I reckon they've spoilt my suit.'

The men tried to take Kidnew to a nearby tram stop, but during the short walk, he fell unconscious, and he was taken to the nearest house, where an ambulance was sent for. It quickly arrived, and the impulsive, naive Kidnew was taken to the Royal Infirmary, where he would stay for over a month. On his arrival at the hospital, Kidnew's suit was removed, and it was with shocked incredulity that the doctors found him to have been the victim of 100 razor cuts, which had drained him of most of his blood. The sheer fact that he had made it to the hospital alive was something of a marvel, and from this point onwards, Frank Kidnew would be the man who had survived 100 slashes and had even joked about his suit being ruined.

Although angry at Kidnew's refusal to follow orders, George Mooney could not hide his admiration for him and made sure that his henchman wanted for nothing during his long stay in hospital. His gang may be outnumbered three to one by the Park Brigade, but with men like Frank Kidnew at his side, he was beginning to like those odds.

The previous arrest of Peter Winsey, and the subsequent attack on Frank Kidnew had been detrimental to the wellbeing of both gangs, as the threat of gang violence was very much in the public eye, and as such, was also very much at the forethought of the local police chiefs. This was no longer a case of a few men scrapping outside an illegal gambling den; it was a co-ordinated and potentially deadly battle.

In the 1920s there was very little in the way of police intelligence and the force was mostly made up of constables whose job it was to break up fights and catch criminals. Therefore, any kind of preventative methods were unlikely, and the police could only wait until the gangs stepped out of line again, and hope that they could collar as many of the troublemakers as they could whilst in the act. The number of constables on the beat had been increased, but Park Hill and West Bar still remained no-go areas, unless a mass police presence could be organised. A single beat policeman would not last longer than a few minutes in these areas without risking life and limb. Sheffield was slowly becoming a war zone, and there was very little that could be done about it without a vast investment in bolstering the police force. However, the country was still in a depression following the ruinous First World War, and money was just not available for the public sector. Despite appealing to senior police staff and local MPs for more funding, the under siege Sheffield Police were simply told to do more with the resources they already had, and therefore refused to risk the lives of the constables already at their disposal.

There followed a few weeks of relative quiet, where no pitched battles were fought, and no serious assaults launched. The gangs had returned to their respective ventures, the Park Brigade concentrated on the Sky Ring, and the Mooney Gang moved back into the race tracks, making a modest sum at the expense of the legitimate bookmakers. As long as there was quiet in the city, the two rival armies were left to their own devices. The police had no appetite to stir up a wasps' nest, and kept an eye out on the gangs from a distance, just to make sure that nothing more serious was occurring.

Unfortunately, this sense of calm was not to last, as neither Mooney nor Garvin were willing to back down. The brief period of inactivity was very much the calm before the storm, as both men racked their brains to think of ways to strike out at the enemy. This was an enforced lull in action, as wounds were tended and troops gathered. The next punch thrown would have to be a knockout blow, and to win the battle, one of the kings would have to be taken.

Chapter 3

The Shift of Power

'It is well if you go in for revenge to make it as complete as possible.'

Robert Barr, British-Canadian Author (1849–1912)

W hen the silence was eventually broken, it was broken so loudly that most residents of West Bar were woken from their sleep. It was 1am on 16 Saturday and the gang violence, which many had hoped was a thing of the past, exploded back into life. The war of attrition was over, to be replaced by very real conflict, and very real weapons. Moments after the loud bangs awoke the neighbourhood, a call was made to the police from a terrified woman, who pleaded with the switchboard operator to send as many men as possible, and as quickly as possible, to 23 Corporation Street, which just happened to be the home of George Mooney and his family.

On arriving at the property, the police were confronted with a number of Park Brigade members, who were throwing rocks at the windows and screaming at Mooney to come out and face them. Bullet holes had perforated the exterior walls, and also one of the members of the Park Brigade, George Ganner Wheywell, who was slumped in the gutter, being tended to by two of his cohorts. Ganner (who had earned his nickname from an unusual way of speaking; 'I'm ganner do this ... ganner do that') was scooped up by two police constables who quickly realised that he would live, having been lucky enough to see both bullets enter his upper arm and the rest of the rescue party managed to fight their way past the remaining Park Brigade, before gaining entry into the house.

On entering, which took some time as the door was heavily barricaded, the constables were confronted by the sight of a hysterical woman, screaming with fright at what had gone on around her. Mrs Mooney was in an acute state of shock and could only point to the back parlour, where George Mooney cowered behind a heavy dresser, having moved into the back room to escape the bullets which had been fired through the broken windows.

Having dispersed the gaggle of onlookers from the street (the majority of Park Brigade had made themselves scarce as soon as the police began their charge), the police summoned an ambulance for Wheywell, and arranged for the Mooney family to be removed from the premises, and into more secure surroundings. George Mooney refused the offer however, and asked for his family to be taken to the home of his older brother. Mooney himself was unable to join them, as the bullet wounds to Wheywell meant that somebody had some serious questions to answer, and that someone would seem to be George Mooney. He was taken into custody for the remainder of the weekend, and remained silent as he was mercilessly questioned about the goings-on of the evening in question.

By Monday morning, the police had been able to request a warrant to search 23 Corporation Street, which was summarily granted by the duty magistrate. Upon first inspection, it would appear that there was nothing unusual about this family home, but when a large heavy chest of drawers was forced open, the search team began to shout with joy. A large cache of weapons had been discovered, and George Mooney was sure to be locked up for a long time. In the house, the police found a double-barrelled shotgun, a hunting rifle, an American revolver, and several knives and coshes. This was the kind of haul that could see a troublemaker like Mooney in a serious amount of trouble, and every effort was taken to catalogue and confiscate every weapon. Surely even an experienced criminal like George Mooney could not talk his way out of this situation?

When confronted with the evidence, Mooney took full responsibility for the shotgun and rifle, stating that he had to defend himself, as he had been victim to threats of violence for the last few weeks, and would do everything in his power to protect his wife and young children. As for the revolver, knives and coshes, he fell back on the same words uttered by thousands of guilty parties over the years 'I have never seen those before, they must have been put there by somebody.'

Mooney was taken back to the cells for the rest of the day, where he would, one by one, be joined by his gang members. The police had taken the opportunity to eradicate the whole gang from being a nuisance to the city once and for all, and were determined to make as many charges as possible, in the hope that at least a few of them would stick. The next morning, the motley crew were brought before the magistrate. In the dock were: George Mooney, 33, of Corporation Street; John Thomas Mooney, 41, of Old Street; Peter Winsey, 38, of Furnace Hill; John Spud Murphy, 38, of Steelhouse

Lane; Albert Foster, 33, of Park Hill Lane; and Thomas Rippon, 34, who lived with John Mooney.

All six of the men were charged with being in possession of a firearm without a licence. This was mainly due to Mooney's reluctance to name any of his cohorts, or name the guilty party who had procured the weapons in question. Spud Murphy was also charged with assaulting a police officer during the first Corporation Street incident, from which he had made a quick getaway.

The proceedings were adjourned until the following week, and it was with great surprise that the magistrate found himself being asked by all the defendants, apart from Thomas Rippon, if they could remain in custody. Obviously confused by the strange request, the magistrate agreed that the men would remain in custody, and left the bench, only to quickly jog back and tell Thomas Rippon that he was free to go as long as he met his bail conditions. Rippon was something of a fringe member of the gang, having been introduced to George by his older brother. He was a reliable enough sort, but never really seemed to relish the violence and cruelty that came with the lifestyle. As such, Mooney was loath to use him as extra muscle unless he had no choice in the matter.

It was probably due to this tenuous link with the gang that Rippon thought himself safe in the streets of Sheffield, but within minutes of his release, he must have wished that he was securely behind bars with the rest of the gang. He had made a serious error of judgement, and would be lucky to escape the vicinity of the courthouse with his life. Waiting outside were the injured Ganner Wheywell, along with several more junior members of the Park Brigade. Wheywell was still furious about the injuries inflicted upon him, and had lain in wait with his young protégés to see which of the Mooney Gang would be foolish enough to stride out of the courthouse and into the open streets. Spotting Wheywell, Rippon immediately bolted up Castle Street, sprinting as fast as his legs could carry him until he reached the Central Police Station, where he threw himself at the mercy of the desk sergeant, and asked to be taken into protective custody alongside the rest of the gang. No sooner had the sergeant opened his mouth to reply, the doors once against burst open, and in came Wheywell, followed by his gang of youths. It was only the presence of several constables in the foyer of the police station that saved Rippon from receiving an almighty beating at the hands of his tormentors. It took several minutes for order to be resumed, during which time most of the chasing gang had been on the receiving end of several hefty truncheon blows.

Rippon was removed under protection back to the cells beneath the courthouse, and the attacking party were all taken in by the police. All but Wheywell would be released the same day, such was their youth and lack of criminal history, but their Ringleader would find himself in the same dock in which Rippon had appeared just a few hours earlier. Wheywell was to stand before the magistrate the very next morning. Charged with assault, Wheywell seemed in carefree spirits as he appeared in the dock. The charge against him was simple enough, but on this occasion, the commander of the Central Police Station, Superintendent Hollis, had chosen to address the magistrate himself, appealing to the bench to keep Wheywell in custody, and voicing his concerns about the growing gang violence within the city. The magistrate, exasperated at the perceived over exuberance of the Superintendent obviously disagreed. 'A good idea' he said, 'would be for them all to go into a field and clear (the feud) up,' before dismissing Wheywell with a nonchalant wave of the hand. One can only imagine the fury of the Superintendent to be ignored in such a way in front of Wheywell, and the rest of the Park Brigade who cheered from the public gallery.

Friday 22 June was the date set for the Mooney Gang to appear collectively before the Crown Court. The charges against all six men were still applicable, as nobody had yet come forward to claim responsibility for the small arsenal at the home of George Mooney. Mr J.W Fenoughty, defending, immediately submitted a guilty plea on behalf of Mooney, and not guilty pleas on behalf of the rest of the gang.

It was not long before the proceedings started to take a farcical turn. The first witness, a man named Pope, had seemingly gone missing since arriving at the court just a few hours before. A search party was sent around the building and up and down the nearby streets, but the man who had volunteered to identify the gang and their criminal behaviour, had simply disappeared.

Mr A.W. Forsdike, prosecuting, and without the services of his first witness, seemed to be a little at sea, but soon composed himself enough to address the judge, telling the tale of events between the rival gangs, and highlighting the detrimental effect this was having on those unlucky enough to live in the vicinity of either gang.

A serving police officer, Detective Inspector Naylor, was called for the defence and admitted that in the three weeks before the attack on his home, Mooney had asked repeatedly for police protection, such were the threats made against him by 'persons unknown', which had been dismissed as it was made clear that a man like Mooney should be able to look after himself.

Another policeman, who had attended the house in Park Hill where Frank
Kidnew was taken after his brutal attack, gave evidence of the brutality he
saw levied against Kidnew that day, and remarked that he often worked in
the vicinity of Park Hill, and that 'even us constables don't go right in to the
centre of Park Hill, it's too dangerous'.

With all seriousness, Mr Fenoughty turned to the judge and stated, 'there
can be no doubt about the assault on Kidnew, and that is the reason that Mr
Mooney and company went into retirement.' This was greeted by howls of
laughter from the public gallery, where several of the junior members of the
Park Brigade sat, watching their enemies being forced to admit their fear in
front of everyone present.

However, it would be Mooney and his gang who would have the last
laugh, as with no evidence against the five gang members, they were allowed
to leave the court with their charges dismissed, and George Mooney, who
had freely admitted to procuring some of the firearms was fined £10, and his
weapons confiscated and destroyed. Before he could leave the courtroom,
Spud Murphy was called back into the dock on a charge of assault against
a police officer. It was alleged that Murphy had thrown a brick which had
injured PC Cranswick during the first altercation on Corporation Street.
Murphy denied the charges, before cheekily adding 'I would have been
delighted to see a policeman's uniform that day'. He was also fined £10, and
allowed to rejoin the rest of the gang who waited outside the courtroom.

This time, the men could leave the court without too much hesitation,
as the main members of the Park Brigade had now had to face their turn in
custody, having been rounded up the previous day to answer the charges
brought against them in relation to the siege upon Mooney's house. The
fines were immediately paid in cash by Mooney, who then led his men from
the courthouse, stopping only briefly to stare at the junior Park Brigade
members who watched them from across the road. Without the main men
to back them up, the youths quickly walked away in the opposite direction.

The case against the Park Brigade was heard on Monday 25 June, just
three days after their rivals had been allowed to walk free. This time, there
were five men in the dock to answer charges of 'unlawfully and tumultuously
assembling outside 23 Corporation Street and behaving in a disorderly
manner', which seems like something of an understatement given the bullet
holes which now decorated the front of the Mooney house. Prosecuting was
Mr A.W. Forsdike once again, and he repeated his speech of the previous
Friday in which he detailed the rivalry between the gangs, and the negative
effect this warfare was having on the people of Sheffield. This time,

Superintendent Hollis did not bother to turn up, knowing that anything he said would once again fall upon deaf ears.

In the dock were George Wheywell of Duke Street, William Furniss of Duke Street Lane, Gilbert Marsh and Albert Flaherty, both of Hoyle Street, and Ernest Chapman of Arundel Street. The five men spent the early part of the proceedings looking bored and grinning at their friends in the public gallery; that is, until the main witness was called to the stand.

The five bristled visibly as George Mooney was called to the witness box. This went against everything that gang culture stood for. It was unthinkable for a gang member, let alone a gang boss to assist the police. Yet, it was without hesitation that Mooney climbed the steps into the box, and stared Ganner Wheywell straight in the eye before he swore his oath on the Bible. Mooney would tell the court that had been unable to leave his house for days upon end due to the threats he was receiving from the Park Brigade, and went on to describe the events of the evening. Wisely, he refrained from including the fact that he had shot Wheywell twice and also did not mention the large number of weapons stashed away in his house. Mr Forsdike then allowed Mooney to leave the stand, and addressed the judge. He stated that there could be no doubt that the Park Brigade were the guilty party on this occasion, and questioned as to what possible reason they could have had for being in West bar in the early hours of the morning, given that none of them lived there. It was plain to see, he added, that the only reason for their trip to West Bar was to attack George Mooney.

Defending the Park Brigade was Mr Irwin Mitchell, whose name still exists on the Sheffield legal scene to this very day, as a branch of solicitors is now named after him. Mitchell called Mooney back to the stand, and with no hint of irony, suggested that it was rather unusual for Mooney to appear in a witness box, especially as how one of his clients had been shot twice, and the only man who could have done it was standing in front of him as a witness for the prosecution. When asked how Wheywell could have been shot if Mooney was not the guilty party, the gang leader grinned at Wheywell, and said, 'I can only assume that it was a bad shot on their part!' Quickly realising that he would get nothing more than attempted comedy from Mooney, Mitchell then called another witness to the stand.

A detective sergeant was next to climb the steps, and consulted his notebook as he went on to give his version of events. He claimed that he had attended Wheywell while he was slumped in the gutter, and the stricken man had told him 'George Mooney has done it', which everybody in the court already knew, but could not prove. Claiming it was very much a case of 'the pot calling the kettle black' and that 'to find the Mooneys here today, in their present capacity, with the police ranged alongside them and Mr Forsdike taking up cudgels on their behalf' was a strange situation indeed. Mitchell was understandably concerned that his clients had not received a fair trial, especially as a man who had shot at them had played a part in the case against them.

After consideration, the judge informed the court that he was determined to take every step available to him to aid in preventing this kind of behaviour from happening again. Yet, it was with a sigh from the prosecution, that another lenient sentence was handed down. Each of the five men were bound over to keep the peace for 12 months, and fined £20 each. The total punishment did not even amount to a day's takings at the Sky Ring.

Wheywell was instructed to remain in the dock whilst the rest of his fellow defendants were allowed to leave. He was to be tried for the assault of Thomas Rippon in the Central Police Station, and once again went back to folding his arms and looking bored and disinterested. However, the police had put two and two together, and added a little extra content to the evidence brought against him. The assault of Thomas Rippon could not be denied, taking place, as it did, in front of a number of police constables and several members of the public. Yet, there were reasons to believe that Wheywell was also one of the leading aggressors in the horrific attack upon Frank Kidnew, who had refused to prosecute. This revelation made Wheywell stand up straight in the dock, and caused more than a few whispers in the public gallery.

The Mooney Gang had the privilege of sitting in the gallery on this occasion, and as the evidence against Wheywell mounted up, the court was shocked as Rippon shouted from above 'I don't want anything to do with it, just let him go'. Whether done out of fear or in adherence to the criminal code of conduct, Rippon had saved Wheywell from a lengthy prison sentence. The man who had subjected Frank Kidnew to 100 slashes of a razor walked free, and had nothing to say in response to his last-minute reprieve. His reputation was now further bolstered by the reluctance of the Mooney Gang to testify against him, and the description of the horrific injuries meted out to Kidnew gave a whole new gravitas to this once lowly thug.

The peace was kept for a little over two hours, as the same afternoon, a troop of mounted police were sent to Park Hill Lane, the street to which Mooney Gang member Albert Foster had inexplicably moved the previous year. The violence had erupted once again, and it would seem that the Park Brigade had taken little notice of the precautionary sentences handed out to them that same morning. However, Sam Garvin, who was always known to play his hands wisely, had forbidden any of the five defendants from taking part in the afternoon's events, and sent a number of his junior members along to Park Hill Lane in order to 'give Foster a nice welcome home'. Garvin, as usual, was the ringleader and main aggressor, but had been canny enough to keep himself out of the dock, and would extend that same honour to those who had taken part in the siege on Mooney's house.

The altercation came out of the blue, as a group of women stood in the street chatting about the morning's events in court. The conversation stopped as they saw a group of around ten men descending upon the house. Screaming to Mrs Foster to take cover and warn her husband, the women tried in vain to halt the group of main, shouting that they had had enough of the violence in the neighbourhood. The men tried in vain to gain entry to the house, where Foster and his wife cowered for dear life. In the meantime, a number of other local women had arrived and argued with the women of Park Hill Lane that they had assisted the Mooney Gang by alerting Foster and giving him chance to barricade the door. Before long, another fight had broken out between the local women, and one woman was taken to hospital having received a nasty gash to the forehead courtesy of a potato masher. Foster was removed from the house by the police, and surrounded by a protective human barrier which accompanied him all the way to West Bar, where he would be joined by his wife at the home of John Mooney, who seemed to be getting used to housing the waifs and strays of the gang. Another serious assault had been averted, but it was becoming clear that very few places were safe for the members of the Mooney Gang.

Despite their status as victims, the Mooney Gang were once more hauled before the magistrate, who informed the men that, as the Park Brigade had been bound over to keep the peace, it was only fair that the same apply to Mooney and his men. The same £20 surety was demanded of each man, and it was with a sense of extreme injustice that the men returned home to West Bar that night.

The next day, Mooney and his five associates made an unexpected appearance back in court, where they quietly sat through proceedings until the magistrates and public could ignore their presence no longer. Waiting for the current dull case to end, Mooney and his men eventually found the right time to approach the Bench, and it was Albert Foster who took the lead on this occasion. He complained to the magistrate that some of them were unable to produce the £20 required for them to be bound over. Unexpectedly, he received the response, 'the other men managed to find it, so you should be able to as well' to which he brazenly replied, 'there are 500 of them on the other side, there are far more of them than there are of us!'

Recognising that they would get no joy from the magistrate, Mooney led his men away from the Bench, but not before Spud Murphy turned to address the court and shouted, 'back Carpathius today and you'll be alright!' before enquiring of the magistrate if the money could be paid the next day. The magistrate agreed, but warned the gang that if the money was not paid by the time the court closed the next day; all six of them would be sentenced to three weeks in prison in default of the payment. As it turned out, Carpathius won in the 3.10, and all fines were paid the next morning. One can only wonder how many of those present in court the previous day took the advice of Spud Murphy.

With all of the main protagonists, apart from Sam Garvin, having been bound over to keep the peace, life in Sheffield became very quiet for a time. The gangs were still in operation, but had wisely decided to stick to their money-making schemes, rather than waste their time and resources in battling each other. The chaos which had ensued in court, and the subsequent fines handed out by the judge were the talk of the town over the coming weeks. It seemed to the ordinary man, that both factions were untouchable, and this created a widespread sense of anger and hopelessness amongst those whose lives had been adversely affected by the Mooney Gang and the Park Brigade.

This mood was reflected by the police force, who found themselves impotent in the fight against the gangs. They could round the thugs up until the cows came home, but if the magistrates were too frightened or lazy to take any proper action against them, their hard work was all in vain. Therefore, the streets of Park Hill and West Bar were again deserted by the police, and the gangs left to their own devices to make whatever illegal money they could, and carry on with their criminal activities without fear of intervention. With all of their top men just an affray charge away from receiving a custodial sentence, the duties of both gangs now fell to the younger, less experienced members. This was an education to many, especially keen young men like Wilfred and Lawrence Fowler, who had eventually been trusted to perform some minor jobs for the Park Brigade.

The quiet was almost disconcerting as the gangs lay dormant, yet the void was filled by other voices, namely those of the police and the press, who took the opportunity to spread the word that the light punishments handed out to the gangs could not be allowed to happen again. The best time to attack a lion is as it sleeps, and that is exactly what the press chose to do.

Chapter 4

Sheffield under Siege

'People who don't expect justice don't have to suffer disappointment.'

Isaac Asimov, Russian-American Author (1920–1992)

E ver since the first gangs had been formed in the city almost a century before, the Sheffield police had developed a knack for staying out of their affairs. Rather than a tactic borne of fear or laziness, this was simply an acceptance of the meagre resources and manpower at their disposal. There simply weren't enough men to stand up to the gangs which seemed to swell in number with each passing incident. Yet, by the time the Mooney Gang and the Park Brigade wrought havoc on the streets, the police force had evolved into something like the modern service we are familiar with today. They were no longer 'crushers' or 'bluebottles'; even the constables were subject to rigorous training and had to meet certain criteria before being allowed onto the force. With their intake of experienced detectives and keen constables, the managing of the gang situation should have been simpler than it had ever been before. Add to this the invention and wide use of the telephone and the handful of cars available to the police, and mobilising the troops against the gangs would have been something that could be organised at relatively short notice.

However, despite having found themselves with the tools to engage the street thugs in battle, the police were still considerably undermanned and with the country being in the financial state brought on by the crippling costs of the war, the investment in public services had all but stopped, and without any kind of danger money to persuade the policemen to take on the gangs, this kind of duty was undertaken by only the bravest of souls.

This isn't to say that the majority of the police were lazy or cowardly; they performed their duties admirably in every other respect, but found themselves outthought and outmanned by the gangs on nearly every occasion. They also found themselves battling against another faction on most instances; a faction that should have been their greatest ally, but seemed to be nothing more than a hindrance to them in their tireless work.

The rise of the post war gangs seemed to have coincided with a rise in apathy by the judicial system. This was a time where a judge or magistrate was, to all intents and purposes, free to deliver whatever punishment they saw necessary, and only in the case of a death sentence would there be any kind of review. Simply speaking, those on the business side of the Bench were free to give themselves an easy life. The speech delivered to the judge by Superintendent Hollis in which he pleaded that the gangs were in control, and only more severe punishment could halt their growth, only to find himself being summarily ignored, was becoming something of a regular event across the nation, with the Sheffield judiciary appearing to be the worst of a bad lot.

It had long been suspected that there were members of the bar employed by the gangs, who delivered lenient sentences in exchange for money, or under the threat of violence. This was never proven, but would go some way to explaining the shockingly light punishments meted out to the gang members on the majority of occasions. A twelve-month binding order for opening fire on a dwelling place was as preposterous then as it is now, and one can only imagine the sentence that would have been imposed if the house in question had belonged to a judge or councillor. Yet, it was almost impossible for this thorny subject to be addressed officially, as to do so would be to accuse the judiciary of corruption and gross misconduct.

The head of the Sheffield Police force at the time was Chief Constable Lt Col John Hall-Dalwood, a man who was no stranger to a battle, having served in the military for the majority of his life and seen action as an officer in the Boer War. Hall-Dalwood seemed the perfect fit for the struggling force, and had been in office for just over a decade before he came to the decision that the current situation was simply untenable. To highlight just how understaffed the police were in Sheffield, official figures show that they had just over 500 men to police a population of half a million. Leeds and Manchester, both with populations less than double that of Sheffield; both had almost three times as many serving police officers at their disposal. To add to the obvious problem, it was also a well-known fact that the gang situations in Leeds and Manchester were nowhere near as serious as those in Sheffield, a city which had been awarded the infamous moniker of 'Little Chicago', such was the level of control enjoyed by the gangs of the long-suffering city. The comparison to the Chicago mafia in the age of prohibition and the murderous reign of Al Capone may have been a little strong, but in terms of the British gang problem, Sheffield was very much a city with a terrible reputation.

To be nationally recognised as a gang-friendly city was nothing short of an embarrassment to Hall-Dalwood and his men. Yet it was a common opinion amongst the criminal fraternities that 'Sheffield had the best judges', although, the general public and those trying to protect them would certainly disagree with this mocking statement. As well as failing to deal with the gangs, Hall-Dalwood was well aware that another problem faced by his men was that they were forced to deal with the anger felt by the general public. Every day, an influx of complaints would be received concerning the failure to apprehend gang members, or the reluctance of the police to patrol the worst affected areas.

It was with gang violence in full swing that Hall-Dalwood made a difficult decision and less than a week after William Furniss had been dragged from his bed and beaten half to death by the Mooney Gang, that the Chief Constable decided to go public with his concerns, something which was unheard of in those days. To speak the truth was to criticise the judiciary, but the time for protecting reputations and saving blushes had long since passed. Hall-Dalwood was also now in possession of a valuable ally, with a statement being made in Whitehall that echoed his own feelings, and made the uneasy task of challenging the legal system slightly more palatable.

The Home Secretary, Viscount Bridgeman, had asked Inspector of the Constabulary Herbert D. Terry, to produce a report on the current state of policing in the country. The report was honest and hard-hitting, and was delivered to the House of Commons just days before Hall-Dalwood made his own statement, which was given Terry's personal blessing. To make the situation known as widely as possible, it would be necessary to bypass the string of council meetings and judiciary reports. He had to reach as many people as possible in order to gain support from the city he had tried so hard to serve, whilst being underfunded and shorthanded for the majority of his tenure.

The report delivered to the House of Commons had bluntly stated that year upon year, it was become less viable for the local police forces to keep order within their boundaries. The most important duties of preventing crime and dealing with those who offended had been severely affected by the number of other duties a police officer was now expected to perform. It was also openly announced that the punishments handed out by all courts, from the local magistrate to the Old Bailey, had become far too lenient, and that the reluctance of the judiciary to levy stricter punishments was something which must be investigated. However, the statement was met with a largely silent response in the House of Commons.

The ruling families and the judicial families were so intertwined that there would be very few who sat in either House that would not have a member of the judiciary either in their family, or in their circle of friends. It was accepted that the police were having a tough time, but the investigation into the courts made most of those present squirm uneasily in their seats. Yet the silence had been broken, and the facts had been presented publicly. This small victory was very much the catalyst for Hall-Dalwood's own response, which was given by way of an interview in the *Sheffield Daily Telegraph*, printed on 7 May and was greeted with agreement from the majority of Sheffield's population:

> 'The public of Sheffield is paying rates for police protection, which under the circumstances, it cannot possibly get. In Sheffield, we have to admit that we are floating on very thin ice indeed, and we also have to admit that, unless more generally helped by punishments to fit crimes, unpalatable as that may be, that Sheffield's police force is utterly inadequate numerically to cope with the wave of crime that must necessarily follow in the wake of the unemployment situation at the present time.
>
> 'It is the boast of the bad man that he gets the best run for his money in Sheffield. He would rather be caught in Sheffield than in any other part of the country because, he says, you have to produce more evidence for the prosecution in a Sheffield court to get a conviction than in any other town in the country.
>
> 'Moreover, the convicted man in Sheffield is invariable pleasantly surprised by the light character of his sentence. What is happening is that we are making thieves.'

On the subject of releasing those who had committed offences, Hall-Dalwood was equally outspoken, challenging the judiciary to think twice before granting bail to those who had been charged with violent or serious offences:

> 'Bail, in my own personal opinion, is being so freely granted that what is happening now is that criminals are laughing in the face of the police, saying that when they are arrested the magistrates will give them bail, and in more cases than one, they have immediately gone away and committed the offence the very same evening.

'If the Sheffield police is to be made more effective, criminals
will have to be far more seriously dealt with by local magistrates,
bail will have to be less readily granted, and the Government will
have to treat the police less like a pack horse for 101 little things
which are outside the province of police duties, and inside that of
Government departments.'

As powerful and honest as his interview was, it would seem that the *Sheffield
Daily Telegraph* was less convinced by his words than the general public were,
as the following editions over the next week contained articles disagreeing
with Hall-Dalwood, and bemoaning a small percentage of people who had
found themselves wrongly convicted over the previous decade. An article
produced in direct response to Hall-Dalwood's statement was also a scathing
attack on his opinions, even going as far as to say that 'leaning on the side
of mercy is not on the whole the worst of faults', which was a sentiment
designed to appeal to the good nature of the Sheffield residents, but merely
ended up pleasing the gang members and other morally bankrupt characters.
In true tabloid style, the newspaper then ran another story six weeks later,
which complained about the levels of violence currently being experienced
in the city, claiming that 'local gangs' were making the streets a dangerous
place to be. However, the article went on to play down the seriousness of the
current situation:

'[The gang problem] has perhaps been over-exaggerated in some
quarters and there is a noticeable tendency to attribute the slightest
breach of the peace to activities of one gang or another. It is this
difficulty in getting hold of the deliberate promoters of real trouble
that has necessarily handicapped police investigations.'

So, to paraphrase the *Sheffield Daily Telegraph*, there was a gang problem,
but it wasn't that bad, and the failure to put a stop to this problem was
on the part of the police who failed to capture the right criminals. Hall-
Dalwood was seething, and rightly so. If the *Telegraph* were not going to take
the matter seriously, the perhaps their main rival, the *Sheffield Mail*, would.
Having met with an experienced *Mail* reporter, Hall-Dalwood was assured
that this particular publication stood by him, and would do everything in
their power to assist in cleaning up the streets. The feature copied below,
under the headline of 'Scandal of Sheffield's Gang Feuds' would suggest
that they were as good as their word:

'The complete failure of the police authorities to crush the lawlessness of the Mooney gang and its rival demands the very earnest consideration of (1) the Chief Constable, (2) the Watch Committee, and (3) the Justices of Peace. We make no attempt at this stage to apportion responsibility.

'As to (1) we assume that the Chief Constable has kept the Watch Committee fully informed about the ramifications of the two gangs. We assume too that he made specific representations to the committee about the manifest need for a special detective organisation.

'As to (2) we assume that the Watch Committee have the fullest confidence in the Chief Constable's ability to create this special organisation and to personally direct it.

And as to (3) we assume that the J.Ps, in the continued and deplorable absence of a virile Stipendiary Magistrate are prepared to give the Watch committee and the Chief Constable the utmost possible support.

'The people of Sheffield have the right to expect that this difficult but quite unexceptionable piece of work shall be done. If it is not done quietly and efficiently, according to the best traditions of English civil government, then the person or persons executively responsible for the failure must go.'

In response to the article, Hall-Dalwood was invited to comment, and used the publicity to assure the public that his force were doing everything in their power to break the gangs, but due to certain factors, the task was being made more difficult by the day:

'I am of the opinion that we are doing all we possibly can to check this sort of thing. The only thing I can do is either prevent crime being committed, or when it is committed, find out the guilty parties. The fact that this is being done is proved by the fact that certain people were brought before the court. What powers we have we are exercising.'

The riposte spoke volumes in that it carefully explained that the Ringleaders of the gangs had been brought before the court, but were given lenient sentences and allowed to go back to their criminal ways. As Hall-Dalwood rightly points out, it is the police's job to get the criminals into court, it is not their job to try and to imprison them. The fact that on most occasions, the gang members were unwilling to testify against each other, was also a major problem. It was all very well the police arresting the perpertrators, but when the victims decided not to press charges in order to stick to their unspoken criminal code, there was absolutely nothing that could be done to salvage the situation.

In allowing the *Mail* to run the story, Hall-Dalwood had been forced to sell his soul slightly, and had allowed his own force and his superiors to be criticised. It is perhaps for this very reason that his tenure as Sheffield's head of police was not to last for much longer. He had traded solidarity for honesty, something which would not be taken lightly in the public service.

By the time the other parties named in the damning *Sheffield Mail* article were asked to give comment, there had been an escalation of the violent attacks between the gangs. Frank Kidnew had been sliced to within an inch of his life, Corporation Street had been witness to two major outbreaks of lawlessness, and Ganner Wheywell had been shot twice and had committed an assault whilst inside a major police station. Yet the head of the Watch Committee, Alderman Alfred Cattell, had no time for what he believed to be the sensationalism of recent events. When pressed by a *Sheffield Mail* reporter, he bluntly stated that he 'never looked' at their newspaper, and doubted that the press was in any way competent to say what should be done about the gang problem. Cattell did grudgingly concede that the gangs were 'a rough lot' but refused to be drawn into the conversation any further, and declined to add any more comment, stating that 'the fewer times Alfred Cattell's name appears in print, either personally or as head of the Watch Committee, the better!' The *Mail* got just as much co-operation from Cattell's deputy, A.J. Bailey, who refused to give the slightest piece of information away. 'I shall not say anything about it here,' he said, 'what I have to say will be said at the Watch Committee meeting.' This was the grand sum of the assistance given by the national body responsible for overseeing the operation and effectiveness of the police forces.

Without the political insight of the Watch Committee, the reporter was charged with finding alternative sources to quote, and found his story by arranging interviews with several local magistrates, who, surprisingly, proved to be much more useful and forthcoming than their counterparts on the Watch Committee. The story made the front page of 26 June edition of the *Sheffield Mail*, and did little to garner any support for the judiciary; such was the ineptitude which spewed forth from at least one of them. It is also noticeable that, as one would expect, the blame, it was suggested, should lie at the door of the police, not the judiciary.

Councillor Moses Humberstone, who was also the leader of the Sheffield Labour Party, was scathing in his attack on the police, but failed to acknowledge that it was he who was charged with imprisoning the gangs, not the police. He put his opinion forth that if such trouble had been caused by gangs of unemployed men, the police would have had no hesitation in bringing an end to it. This suggested that he believed the police to be afraid of the gang members, before suggesting that the miscreants 'should be locked up until we get the whole lot of them in prison', momentarily forgetting that this part of the process was *his* job. His view was also shared by Alderman Wardley J.P., who already had a reputation of being something of a dinosaur in the legal system. He blamed the problems on the police's failure to 'settle' the gangs, before launching into a nostalgic recollection that bore little relevance. 'I remember,' he said, 'fifty years ago there were gangs in the city which could have swallowed up the Mooney Gang.' As if to prove that he had no real idea what he was talking about, Alderman Wardley then went on to speak of the Mooney Gang, without even the slightest inkling of the existence of the Park Brigade, who were, by this point, the main aggressors within the city, and the problem wasn't that the Mooney Gang needed to be 'settled', it was that the Park Brigade 'settling' the Mooney Gang that had caused the rise in gang warfare.

The only magistrate to speak with any honesty or integrity was Mr Harry Fisher J.P, a man who had dealt with individual gang members on several occasions, and had quite a lot to say about the gang problem, and the problems within the judicial system. Of the three men interviewed, Fisher was the only one who seemed to share any empathy with the residents of Sheffield:

> 'The man in the street has been heard to say that both the Watch Committee and the City Council, and even some of the magistrates suffer from 'blue funk'. It is beyond doubt that this local outcry should be more drastically dealt with. Doses of soothing syrup to these delinquents are quite useless.
>
> 'We have on the bench a few JPs who fearlessly grapple with the cases that come before them, but it seems to me that some of the older magistrates possess more pluck than the recent additions to the bench.
>
> 'Unless these gentry are shown – either by broken heads with a policeman's baton, or by lengthy terms of imprisonment – that

they cannot terrorize peaceful citizens, very little progress will be made.'

The following day, the 26 June edition of the *Mail* featured an article written by one of their reporters, which was an attempt to educate those who were unfamiliar with the gangs, and warned of their behaviour. This was very much a public service article, and, wisely, was published without crediting the author:

> 'The leaders of these gangs of Sheffield outlaws and free booters are men who live on the fat of the land. They are men of good appearance. They possess persuasive personalities and glib tongues. They use every possible art and device to carry on their nefarious business.
>
> 'At one moment they spend money as freely as if it was water, the next they are grabbing a glass of beer from a man's mouth. They are a nuisance and a danger to publicans – they break glasses, assault customers, and smash windows, pull their own beer and don't pay for it.
>
> 'They work the confidence trick on inoffensive people, row with one another and demand drinks after closing hours. Everyone goes in fear of them and they know it. One of their pet methods of assault is to break a glass on the counter and attack a man's face with the jagged edges.
>
> 'All kinds of men are employed by the proprietors (of the Sky Ring) to deal with various classes of 'business'. They have glib tongued contricksters who can lay a man out as easily as knocking over a nine-pin. One of the principals has himself been a boxer. Others dress flashily, wear heavy gold watch guards and display their wealth arrogantly.
>
> 'These are not ignorant ruffians. They are men who have calculated quite coolly and calmly the gains to be won by their terrifying outlawry. They are prepared to put up a stiff fight for supremacy. Strong measure will be necessary to beat them down.'

As, at the time of writing, the Mooney Gang was looking all but defeated, it is safe to assume that the article is, in fact, written about the Park Brigade, especially as the 'business' and 'contrickery' is mentioned, and that the ex-boxer Sandy Bowler (aka Charles McKay Barlow) is mentioned in all but name. Nevertheless, this is a very accurate description of the men of both gangs.

Apparently keen to persist in their warnings, the *Mail* then ran another story the next day, which claimed to be based upon information gained from a gang member, in which the newspaper warns of further violence, suggesting that the warring factions were both looking to bolster their numbers, and that assistance may well be called in from further afield:

> 'I am reliably informed that the leader of one of the gangs has been to London to secure the services of a gang whose name is known nationally, and who have been asked to travel to the Northern (race) meetings to offer their support.
>
> 'On the other hand, there is a suggestion that the other gang is taking steps to secure the services of a Birmingham gang.'

The Birmingham gang in question was not the Peaky Blinders, but the Brummagem Boys, who were led by the fearsome Billy Kimber. These were organised and experienced thugs, and the leader of the Park Brigade, Sam Garvin, was well know to Kimber, having met several times on race tracks across the nation during his previous occupation as a registered bookmaker.

Even more frightening was that the gang with which George Mooney was linked was the Sabini Gang, whose leader; Charles 'Darby' Sabini (aka Ottavio Handley) was the sworn enemy of Billy Kimber, having led vicious pitched battles against the Brummagem Boys at race meetings over the past decade. The Sabini Gang were a fearsome prospect, and were well known for their brutality and willingness to think nothing of attacking with a razor or revolver. Had George Mooney been able to garner their support, the shift of power in Sheffield could once again have been turned upon its head.

However, the passage of time proved both predictions to be exaggerated. There were alliances formed on the racetracks, but none which would ever spill into the streets of Sheffield. This was a small mercy indeed, but to assume that the violence would die down would be foolish to say the least.

Chapter 5

The *Mail* and the Mayhem

'All war is a symptom of man's failure as a thinking animal.'

John Steinbeck, American Author (1902–1968)

George Mooney was now in the same position that he had found himself as the war had ended. He had been publicly humiliated, and was forced to battle on the race tracks for a meagre sum. As for his cohorts, only the most loyal remained. The senior gang members still stood by their leader, but the foot soldiers had long since marched in the opposite direction. With very little left to lose, Mooney decided that, if he was on his way out, he would take as many people as possible with him. Once again, he was to break the unwritten code of the criminal fraternity, and take his story to the newspapers, where he would recount the tale of his rise to the top in a detailed and honest manner.

As the *Sheffield Mail* seemed to have the monopoly on all things gang-related, there seemed nowhere better to tell his story. The police had been given their say, as had the magistrates and the politicians. It was time for Mooney to get his name in the papers, perhaps for the final time, and this time, there would be no court report to follow, just a full and frank account of his years as head of the infamous Mooney Gang. Before his meeting with special correspondent J.T. Higgins, Mooney did not breathe a word of his plans to anyone. He knew that, had he informed his cohorts, they would have moved hell and earth to talk him out of it. He also could not risk the Park Brigade finding out, as they would surely use any method possible to stop him. This was the act of a man who had nothing left to lose. He would tell his story to the world, and then find a quiet place to live with his wife and children. In doing so, he would be officially handing control of the city over to the Park Brigade, but as was already painfully obvious, that control had been lost a long time ago.

To begin the interview, Mooney first wanted to set the record straight on a number of things. There were a lot of falsehoods relating to his gang, which most believed to be the gospel truth. With such a scoop having presented itself to him, the reporter had no hesitation in allowing Mooney to begin the meeting by settling his own agenda. The first point that Mooney wished to make, was that his gang and the Park Brigade were completely different types of 'organisation' and to lump the two together was nothing short of ridiculous. 'They talk about two gangs,' he said, 'but there are 100 of the so-called rivals, and only really five of us. That is my brother and me, John Murphy, Albert Foster and Peter Winsey.' This was a lie to begin with as the figures given may have been accurate at that point, but were nothing close to the numbers at his disposal when the gang had been at full force. He failed to mention Thomas Rippon, who had decided that the life of crime was not for him, and Frank Kidnew, who was still recuperating from his horrific injuries. He also failed to mention the fifty or sixty casual 'employees' he had taken on when the Sky Ring was in full swing.

Having said his piece and, in his own mind, set the record straight, the interview proper began, and the first topic was that of the Sky Ring, the business which had sparked the majority of the ensuing conflict, and had for some time kept the Mooney Gang in sharp suits and ready cash. Mooney confirmed that the Sky Ring was where all of the trouble between the two gangs began, stating that it was a well-known fact that the business was doing well, and it was when the Ring was at its peak, that he started to receive threats from some of the men who lived in the Park Hill area. It was these threats, he claimed, in addition to the eventual downturn of fortune at the Ring that had fuelled the creation of the Park Brigade just as he found himself unable to keep on a large proportion of his employees.

He also told the reporter that he believed the threats to be more provocation than serious warnings, insinuating that the Park Brigade wanted him to resort to violence in order for the matter to become so serious that the police would take him away, leaving the Sky Ring unattended:

'They think that if they can get us to slash with razors, or kill, or whatever is to be done – and they are trying hard to provoke trouble – we shall be out of the way, and the park gambling Ring will be left to them and their claim will not be tampered with.

'But, we do not want to slash, and we do not want to interfere with them. There is no need to trouble to put us out. For four years we have been trying to live down the title of the Mooney Gang.'

Mooney then went on to say that many of the crimes attributed to his gang had been nothing to do with them, and had been committed by the hangers-on that always seemed to form at the periphery of the group. He also took this opportunity to rubbish the remarks previously made by the out of touch Alderman Wardley in a previous edition of the *Mail*:

> 'Every time there is a street brawl or these people go threatening or holding up publicans – and it is being done very often – the first thing people say is "it's the Mooney Gang again", although we know nothing about it.
>
> 'Then there is Alderman Wardley for instance, he talks off the top in what he said in the Mail. Does he know who the Mooney gang are? A lot of the real gang (the Park Brigade) come from where Alderman Wardley comes from but I do not blame him for that.
>
> 'It is absurd for him to talk about gangs fifty years ago and mix them up with us. He might be a little less loose.'

The interview ended with a boast which was more in keeping with George Mooney, in which claimed that he could take £200 out of the Sky Ring on most days, and had once taken £1,000, but doubted that the business could turn over that kind of money under its new management.

Lastly, when asked if the revelations he had made during the interview worried him, Mooney responded in a fashion which seemed to be an official announcement of retirement. 'We have no fear of drastic police action,' he said, 'all we want is to be left alone to live in peace.'

The unusual interview was the hot topic around Sheffield over the next few weeks, with many forming their own opinions on the man whose name was synonymous with greed and violence. Whatever Mooney's real reason for allowing the interview, his name was certainly back in the hearts and minds of his fellow townsfolk. The feature had been read with interest by many, but had also received its share of criticism. Many believed that a man like Mooney should not be allowed to use the press for his own agenda, while others held the opinion that not one word uttered by the gang boss was true; he had simply used a public platform to allow himself to walk away without hindrance.

One of the main criticisms came from the *Sheffield Independent*, which had already proven that it would not recognise the power and legitimacy of the gangs in their treatment of John Hall-Dalwood. A rebuttal to the *Mail's* article was printed the very next day, and was scathing in its comments as to whether Mooney was telling a single word of truth:

> 'The spectacle of Satan rebuking sin is always entertaining, and it is an appealing picture which George Mooney paints of the reformed outcasts trying to live down their evil past, but prevented from doing so by the unwelcome attentions of their former - and temporarily victorious – associates.'

However, by this point, a bad review was the least of Mooney's problems. He had made a grave misjudgement in naming his fellow Mooney Gang members so publicly, and Peter Winsey, Spud Murphy, and Albert Foster had taken great exception to this, so much so, that they marched into the *Sheffield Mail* offices the very next morning. They demanded a retraction in which it would be stated that they had been named without cause, and that they had nothing whatsoever to do with the interview, or any of the acts listed within the article. The *Mail* had no problem in printing the retraction, as the journalist had incorrectly assumed that the interview had been discussed with the other members of the gang before being sent to print. As far as George Mooney was concerned, there was no longer a Mooney Gang, a sentiment which was now echoed by his closest allies. They had been publicly betrayed, and would make sure that their former leader was left in no doubt as to their feelings on the matter. This was very much the end for the reformed Mooney Gang.

Nobody was at home when the three called at the Mooney household to remonstrate with George, and it was speculated that he had taken his family and left the area in fear of reprisal. However, this proved to be a false suspicion, as later that afternoon, Spud Murphy came face to face with Mooney as they walked towards each other on Steelhouse Lane, West Bar. A heated argument ensued, and as a group of onlookers rushed towards them, not to break up the row, but to watch in the hope that two gang members would come to blows. One witness reported hearing Mooney shout at Murphy 'this is because of you blackmailing people!' to which Murphy replied 'it's through you coming the cop on in the paper.'

It is believed that the comment about blackmail was due to an argument the two had had some weeks before, when Murphy, unhappy at the lack of action against the Park Brigade had made a threat that they either attack Sam Garvin, or he would go and work for him. The two had endured a fractious relationship ever since. Mooney was first to swing landing a thunderous punch to the mouth which sent Murphy staggering into the wall. However, Murphy was no slouch, and within seconds the two were beating the living daylights out of each other. It was only when two detectives from the nearby West Bar police station arrived to investigate the cause of the melee that order was restored, and the two former friends were taken to the cells to cool down.

They appeared in court on the following Monday, 2 July. The two were charged with a breach of the peace, and were placed in the dock with two burly police men between them. Mooney pleaded guilty, remarking that 'I was going to settle it there and then. I said I was getting away from all my pals, and this was the end of it.'

Murphy, who was probably thinking that he had nobody to pay his fines anymore, pleaded not guilty, insisting that Mooney had 'come upon him like a wild man'. The magistrate was not convinced, and both were bound over for twelve months in the sum of £5 each. This is an important point, as it would seem that nobody in the court was aware, or cared to mention, that the two were already bound over for £20. Something was amiss, and the next case to be heard in the very same courtroom would also indicate that this was to be no oridinary court case. .

It would seem that Murphy and Mooney were not the only two gang members to have had a lively afternoon on the day the article was printed. Foster and Winsey had travelled home together by tram, and were taken by surprise when an unaffiliated local hard man jumped off a different tram travelling the other way, and set about them without warning. The man, Louis Handley, had taken exception to the gang having caused a commotion outside his house the previous week, and was waiting for an opportunity to exact revenge. Foster was knocked unconscious by the first mighty blow, and Winsey sustained a torn ear as Handley had grabbed him before landing a series of further blows. The attack was over within seconds, with Handley walking away but being intercepted by a nearby constable. As such, it was with irony that he was now to be brought before the same magistrate, and would have his case heard directly after that of Mooney and Murphy. However, this is where the similarity ended.

On this occasion, the magistrate had decided that enough was enough, and he sentenced Handley to two months hard labour, the maximum sentence for assault. Again, nobody pointed out the strange contrast in that he had just bound over two gang members with lengthy criminal records for the same kind of offence, but had sent a man with previous good character to prison.

With Spud Murphy having handed in his notice in such a public and explosive fashion, it was only a matter of time before the other members of the dissolved Mooney Gang would officially confirm the split from their erstwhile employer. The next publicly to cut his ties with Mooney was Albert Foster, who appeared, as a witness, in court alongside Frank Kidnew, who was now well enough to be held to account for the earlier disturbance on Corporation Street.

Kidnew had been one of the brawlers in the first West Bar disturbance, and was now sufficiently stitched up and bandaged to be able to stand in the dock. He was charged with kicking PC Sapsford (the poor chap who had also been struck with a brick) outside the home of George Mooney, as the brawl had moved slightly up the road from the house of ill repute. When told by the constable that the offence had occurred outside Mooney's house, the magistrate had asked (one can only assume for purposes of confirmation) who George Mooney was; to which the constable stated that he was a close friend of the defendant. Mr Fenoughty, defending (as always) then made a point of asking, 'Are you sure of it?'

Albert Foster was then called to the witness box, and was immediately asked whether he was a friend of Mooney. 'I was until yesterday,' was the reply. 'I have had a basin full.' This caused great hilarity in the public gallery, which was largely populated by the usual junior members of the park Brigade. Another of Mooney's top men had forsaken him. It must have been music to the ears of Sam Garvin, who found himself in the position of watching his nemesis self-destruct. It was within minutes that another of Mooney's most loyal followers would deny any allegiance to his former employer, as Frank Kidnew was given a chance to speak out via his solicitor. Mr Fenoughty read out a statement made by Kidnew, in which he openly stated that he was not a friend of George Mooney, and had no interest in any business matters of the Mooney Gang. He went on to describe his previous service, both as a reservist, and throughout the entire World War One campaign. He had only been in trouble once for playing football in the street.

When the laughter from the gallery had died down, Fenoughty went on to explain that his client was a widower with four children to provide for, and had been able to save enough money to relocate to Blackpool, where he had been offered a job with an old army pal. This was a clever move, as the fact that Kidnew was removing himself from Sheffield left the magistrate with little appetite to deliver much punishment. As the rest of the men had been, Kidnew was bound over for 12 months in the sum of £20, and immediately left the court room as a man free from further punishment, and also free of George Mooney. It would later transpire that the two men in court that day, were the two who had broken into the home of William Furniss and launched the silent poker attack; on the express orders of George Mooney.

In cutting their ties with the gang, it would seem that both men now lived in hope that their public capitulation would see them free from intimidation by the Park Brigade. They had perhaps been a little over optimistic in this thought, as although Frank Kidnew escaped the mob, Albert Foster was not to be so lucky. On leaving the court, Foster immediately went in search of refreshment, and hailed a cab to the Albert Inn on Sutherland Street. Someone seems to have used the cliché of 'follow that cab', as he had not even taken the first swig of his ale before trouble arrived in the shape of four Park Brigade men.

William Furniss, Ganner Wheywell, Gil Marsh and Charles Price had squeezed into a cab hot on the tail of Furniss' nocturnal attacker. What followed was the kind of savage attack that some of these men were already adept in delivering. But, for once, Albert Foster was firmly on the receiving end, and was lucky to escape with his life. Gil Marsh delivered the first blow, a wild swing with a nearby snooker cue which felled Foster instantly. This was followed up by a kick to the head from Furniss, and a punch from Price. Trying desperately to crawl to safety, Foster was then knocked unconscious by an ashtray swung at the back of his head by Wheywell. It was a cowardly attack. The four men had approached their lone enemy from behind, and inflicted most of the serious injuries as he lay stricken. The cowardice and brutality of the attack was probably the main reason that the landlord did something he would normally have avoided like the plague. He waited for the men to leave, and then called the police, naming the attackers.

The four men were arrested later that day, and were held in the cells until they could be brought before the magistrate the following morning. The brief proceedings which would follow were notable for more than one reason, and it would seem that this was one attack too far for even the judiciary to ignore. Before the case was heard, the magistrate (not the same one who had bound over Frank Kidnew) had complained that the gang cases were becoming something of a circus, and requested a number of plain clothes policemen to keep order. He also instructed that anybody known to be from the Park Brigade be refused entry to the public gallery.

This change in attitude did not bode well for the four assailants, as the long-suffering Mr Forsdike, prosecuting, begged the magistrate to make an example of these men. They had been witnessed assaulting a man mob-handed and without mercy, and two of them had been found to be carrying weapons when later arrested.

Defending, Mr Irwin Mitchell appealed to the court that the attack was due to an even more cowardly assault committed on the sleeping body of William Furniss, and that the feud was naturally dying down, such was the very public dissolution of the Mooney Gang. However, this did little to persuade the magistrate, who sentenced all four men to two months hard labour.

Foster did not wait around to see if the feud would settle down. Within days, he had escaped the Park Brigade (and the maintenance arrears owed to his ex-wife) by relocating to Birmingham, where he immediately sought out Billy Kimber. Knowing that the Mooney Gang had planned to join forces with the Sabinis, Kimber was suspicious at first, but eventually relented, as a battle hardened, experienced gang member was too good a gift to turn away.

George Mooney no longer stepped out in public. He and his family had spent the last few months being barricaded inside their home at 23 Corporation Street. The immediate furore seemed to have died down, but the former gang leader was not taking any chances. His wife occasionally left the house, but Mooney had not seen daylight for quite some time. It came out of the blue then, that at 10pm on a Monday night, the couple were disturbed by a loud banging at the door. The unexpected callers were Peter Winsey and Spud Murphy, who had obviously been drinking, and had chosen this moment to take up their grievances with the elusive George Mooney. There was also a third man present, an older man named William Flynn, who was well known to Mooney.

Winsey had been like a brother to Mooney, and was rightly distraught at being named and shamed in the newspaper. Yet, until now, he had kept his opinions to himself, as he was still firm friends with John Mooney, who had also been named. Spud Murphy was simply a man who loved violence, and had decided to accompany Winsey for a second attempt at fighting Mooney. As for William Flynn, he was Mooney's stepfather, and had always endured a tough relationship with his wife's wayward son. As Mooney peered gingerly through the window, the call was made for him to come out and fight. Tired of the feud, and outnumbered, Mooney withdrew to the back of the house and awaited the inevitable. Moments later, his windows were smashed. Luckily, having had chance to secure his home over the previous weeks, the barricades held, and the Mooneys survived untouched.

Not even his own family could bear to see George go unpunished for turning public informer. The only person who had not sought to inflict violence upon him was his older brother, who was happy enough to let the others fight on his behalf. He was out of the gang life now, and would no longer be in the shadow of his younger brother.

A few weeks later, the psychopathic Spud Murphy sank to an even lower level of cowardly attack. He had spotted Mrs Mooney in the doorway of a friend's house, and told her to bring her husband to him, which she refused. Threatening to smash up the friend's home, Murphy then hit Mrs Mooney with a half brick, knocking her unconscious. Mrs Mooney was six months pregnant at the time. She was lucky to survive the attack, and was taken to hospital where she received a number of stitches in her head wound. Murphy was immediately arrested, and was told by the magistrate that he was to appear before the crown court, such was the repeated and shocking violence that he had inflicted upon the Mooney family.

The judge at the eventual trial had no fear of the gangs, and warned the defence counsel of this before the trial had even begun. His summing up and sentencing of Murphy is very interesting, as one word in the speech speaks volumes, a word that appears in bold and underlined to mark the emphasis placed upon it:

> 'People in the city of Sheffield, be their names Mooney or Murphy or Smith or Jones, or anything else, must know that if they come up to *these* courts and are convicted of crimes of violence, they will be dealt with in a suitable manner. Taking into consideration all the circumstances, you are sentenced to six months hard labour.'

The last notable event of the year took place on Christmas Eve, 1923. After a day of heavy drinking, a group of men chose the season of goodwill to reacquaint themselves with the hermit-like George Mooney, who was tucked up in bed at the time, suffering from influenza. This time, the reinforced doors and windows did not hold. The men had decided to use the back entrance of the house, and their luck paid off, only finding a relatively standard wooden door in their way. It took just a few mighty kicks for the door to come off its hinges, and the assailants had managed to invade the inner sanctum of George Mooney for the first time.

This was indeed an auspicious occasion, as following his two henchmen, Sandy Bowler and Robert Crook into the kitchen, was Sam Garvin, a man who normally went to great lengths in order to keep his own hands clean. If the presence of Garvin was a shock, however, the next man to enter the kitchen was an even bigger surprise. It was Frank Kidnew, now employed by the gang who had left him for dead with 100 deep cuts. Even upon finding the downstairs only inhabited by Mrs Mooney and her four children (one of whom was only ten days old), the men did not stop in their tracks. 'We've come to wish your father a merry Christmas,' Kidnew said chillingly to Mooney's 15-year-old daughter. Luckily for her father, he had heard the commotion, and managed to take the only action available to him in his lone and weakened state.

Hiding in a cupboard was not what would be expected from a former gang boss, but that is exactly what Mooney did. Hearing a shout of 'give him some razor, Frank' as the footsteps on the stairs grew louder, all Mooney could do was to hold his breath and pray that he would not be found. His prayers were answered. Having had the foresight to open the bedroom window before secreting himself in the cupboard, Mooney had managed to fool the attackers into thinking that he had absconded from the house. The men turned on their heels, keen to track down their prey, smashing anything within arm's length that they passed on the way.

The police arrived soon after, and took a statement from the much-tormented Mrs Mooney. By the time that night fell, all four men had been arrested by a hastily assembled army of police constables, and would spend the festivities locked away in the cells of West Bar police station. They would appear in court on 27 December. This was only ever going to be an arraignment hearing, and it was with a foolish sense of bravado that Robert Crook boasted that any one of them could have posted bail even if it was set at £1,000, to which the magistrate to exception, and stated that, had he been able to, he would have taken Crook at his word and set the bail at that amount. However, with his hands tied by bail guidelines, the magistrate could only demand £20 for the bail of each man.

The trial, which took place on 9 January 1924, had been something of a red-letter day on the calendar of many Sheffield residents, especially as it was revealed that George Mooney was to testify against the four attackers. They were expecting a fascinating trial and were certainly not disappointed.

The crowds had been forming since dawn and by the time the court opened for business, there was much pushing and shoving to secure a place in the public gallery. Those who were not able to gain access chose to wait in the chilly weather, hoping to catch a glimpse of George Mooney as he arrived to give evidence. When he did arrive, the crowd was surprised to see and pale and frightened looking man being escorted into the court with a ring of policemen around him. The once-mighty gang lord had been reduced to being a harassed and intimidated witness, who could do nothing more than try to convince the judge that his attackers should not be allowed to walk free.

Samuel Garvin, 38, of Heavygate Avenue; Frank Kidnew, 40, of Campo Lane; Charles McKay Bowler (Sandy Barlow), 32 of Stepney Street; and Robert Crook, 34, of Corporation Street had all been charged with criminal damage. No assault charges were brought, as they had not managed to find Mooney on this particular occasion.

Mooney told his side of the story briefly and honestly, drawing sniggers from the court as he admitted to hiding in a cupboard. He was then cross-examined by Mr Irwin Mitchell, who mentioned that the witness had 53 previous convictions. 'Yes,' replied Mooney with an uncharacteristic smirk, 'but I have never smashed anything!' Mooney's daughter was also called as a witness, and could identify Kidnew and Bowler without any doubt, but was less certain of the involvement of the other two men, as they had both loitered on the periphery of the house without going any further than the kitchen. As such, Garvin and Crook were allowed to leave without charge.

Kidnew and Bowler were not so lucky, and were both warned before sentencing by the judge. 'The police wish me to say that there is only one way of stopping this class of violent behaviour, and suggest that the time has arrived where more severe penalties should be inflicted.'

Both men were sentenced to three months hard labour for the crime of criminal damage, which does seem ironic, as both of them had previously been bound over or fined on many occasions for far more serious offences. Bowler's military career and Kidnew's injuries were not enough to persuade the judge to be lenient, and for a short while at least, Sheffield was free of two of its most dangerous thugs.

As for Mooney, apart from his wife and children, he was entirely alone. His whole gang had turned against him, and even his brother, John Mooney, who could not bring himself to attack his own brother, had emigrated to America in disgust, hoping to find a life where his brother was no longer a millstone around his neck. By the end of the month, the Mooneys had also gone. They had left Sheffield as a family, and had left no clue as to where they would go. Sheffield was now a one-gang city, and a chapter of local history had been closed. However, the story was not to end here.

Chapter 6

The Charge of the Park Brigade

'So few are the easy victories as the ultimate failures.'

Marcel Proust, French Author (1871–1922)

The victorious leader of the Park Brigade had certainly earned his reputation. He had been a major player in the gang cultures of several towns and cities. Yet, like Mooney, Garvin had failed to fight in the First World War; however, rather than deserting, he had simply never been caught in order to be handed his conscription papers. Whether his avoidance of military service was due to his travelling, or his travelling was due to avoidance of military service was never ascertained, but it was probable that Garvin would have settled on the former. Without any proof that he had avoided service, Garvin also avoided the social stigma that came with it.

Over the years, he had been convicted of crimes over the length and breadth of the country. Appearing on the court records in Cardiff, Ripon, Derby, Leicester, Blackpool, Leek, Doncaster, and even the Isle of Man, where he had been imprisoned for a street robbery committed in Douglas, Garvin had certainly had time to learn his trade, and his travels also meant that he had contacts in many places. At the end of the war, he had been a part of George Mooney's gang, and had been well respected by his boss, such were his criminal credentials, and was trusted to handle a number of 'affairs'. Yet, as the new team were replaced by the former gang men especially brought in by Mooney, Garvin had fallen into disfavour, and soon decided to leave the gang in favour of finding his own place in 'Little Chicago'.

Not even Garvin had expected the rise of the Park Brigade to be so successful. At its outset, the plan was merely to assemble enough troops to match those of George Mooney, in order for a serious bid for the Sky Ring to be made. Yet, within weeks, the gang had swelled in number and dwarfed the Mooney Gang. This was the deciding factor in Garvin being able to take the Sky Ring by mere intimidation, rather than having to call a full scale assault.

Unlike Mooney, Sam Garvin was quite a popular man. Those who knew of him were only too aware of his violent side, but also knew him as a man who would regularly organise charity events, and was generous with his time and his money. He even organised a boxing match to raise funds for the families of the miners killed in a pit collapse at the Nunnery colliery, receiving many plaudits in the newspaper. At the time, Garvin had been on bail for the Christmas Eve attack on George Mooney's home.

He was a physically impressive, well-dressed man, as was George Mooney, but there was something about Sam Garvin, he seemed to be able to carry it off more successfully than his rival, who had once been described as looking like 'an ape forced into a Sunday suit'. He bought rounds in pubs, gave to charity, had friends on the council, and treated his men well. If this had been a popularity contest, Garvin would have won hands down. He was also a cannier criminal than Mooney, having successfully managed to keep his name out of every incident bar one throughout the feud. He favoured sending his trusted men in his place, to organise a group of younger, more bloodthirsty, foot soldiers. The only occasion where Garvin had stepped out of the shadows was the Christmas Eve attack, and he would freely admit to the cause of this being a long day of drinking to the festive season. He had been acquitted on that occasion, but was dismayed by the subsequent imprisonment of his right-hand man, Sandy Bowler, and his impressive new addition to the gang, Frank Kidnew. As the Mooney Gang had now ceased to exist, and the courts were beginning to make an example of gang members, Garvin made the decision to keep things nice and quiet for a few months.

Indeed, it was some nine months after his court appearance that Garvin was in the newspapers again. He had been charged with the theft of £100 from a businessman on a train, along with his brother, Robert, long time gang member Gil Marsh, and the recently released Sandy Bowler. All three appeared in court on 23 September 1924.

The case was thrown out, but it would seem that the Park Brigade had ended their period of contemplation, and there were still a few matters to attend to, namely the reluctance of Spud Murphy and Peter Winsey to leave the city in the footsteps of both Mooney brothers and Albert Foster. The fact that they did not feel the need to leave was seen as a slight upon Garvin, and his organisation. Yet it would seem more likely that, as either man could have easily been welcomed in to the Park Brigade, the fact that they hadn't approached Garvin may have been the real reason for his ire. Whatever the reason for his sudden urge to intimidate the stragglers of the Mooney Gang, Garvin wasted no time in sending orders out to his men.

On 8 December, old wounds were reopened, possibly due to the festive season again, and a reminder was sent out to the remaining ex-Mooneys that the city was still in the hands of their former opposition. The plan was well co-ordinated, as it was carried out as the remains of the Mooney Gang had gathered for a pleasant evening together. Spud Murphy and Tommy Rippon, and their respective wives were enjoying an evening listening to the wireless, along with Peter Winsey and another couple. They had gathered at the Rippons' house to spend some time together away from the all-seeing eyes that followed them whenever they walked the streets.

It was getting late, almost 11pm, when a noise was heard outside the house at 31, Furnace Hill. This was followed by the trademark brick through the window. A gunshot then rang out, and the people in the house dived for cover. However, the attack was short lived, as soon after the men outside came clambering through the broken window, the police arrived, having been watching the group of men since they left the city centre. Most of the soiree guests had managed to make it up the stairs to safety where they barricaded themselves in a back bedroom. Ironically, it was the couple, Mr and Mrs Dale, who had no apparent gang ties who bore the brunt of the attack. Mrs Dale had been injured by flying shards of glass, and she could only scream in hysterics as the intruders began to smash up the house, and set about her husband with the legs broken from a stool.

This was the scene that greeted the onrushing police officers. Fortunately, they had arrived in enough number to subdue the intruders without too much of a struggle. In all, five men were arrested, and a few more who had loitered outside had scarpered as they realised they had been followed by the police. One of the constables present was an old hand in dealing with the gangs, and was surprised to see a reprisal of the troubles. Asking the intruders why they had broken the peace after so long, he received the curt reply, 'Just warming up old broth'.

The five men were brought before the magistrate the next morning. Gil Marsh, Sandy Bowler, Ernest Scott, William Wareham and William Carr were all charged with affray. The man who had broken the window, William Wareham, was heavily bandaged around the head and throat. Obviously, his window-breaking skills needed some practice! Among the evidence shown to the Bench were a revolver, a razor, a hatchet, a few coshes, and the stool legs used to attack Mr Dale. The defendants were returned to custody for a further week on order to appear at the Crown Court. However, all were bailed at the initial crown court hearing, as the prosecution had asked for more time to prepare.

The rest of the 1924 festive season was a tawdry mess of tit-for-tat attacks, with members of both the defunct Mooney Gang, and the Park Brigade being victim to amateurish public assaults. This could not go on, as far too much attention was being drawn to the resurgence of gang violence. The man to put his foot down and say enough was enough was Sam Garvin. He had already found himself in the dock due to one drunken farce, and was not going to repeat that mistake any time soon. The frequent attacks by and on his men were drawing a lot of attention from the police and the press, and Garvin had become increasingly annoyed that the childish rivalry was beginning to affect his trade at the Sky Ring.

There were far bigger fish to fry than people like Spud Murphy and Peter Winsey, and Garvin wanted his men to be on the ball, as he concentrated on consolidating his ownership of the Sky Ring, and looked for more lucrative schemes. The desire for a peaceful life led Garvin to do something he had rarely done ever in his life; he would offer a second chance to his enemies.

Garvin reasoned that if the few Mooney Gang stragglers were taken under his wing, then there would be nobody for his men to fight, leaving them to concentrate on the jobs he had given them, namely protecting the Sky Ring and running his affairs at the race tracks. The reconciliation was a success, and even the Mooney men were astonished by his generous olive branch. The ex-Mooney Gang members were not only invited to work at the Sky Ring, but they were also allowed to be on a committee which would decide the sharing out of the profits. This was to be a venture between the two infamous gangs, but without the input of George Mooney. Without him, Garvin believed, there was no reason that the Sky Ring could be not used to everybody's benefit.

This was such big news that the newspapers even reported on this armistice. The New Year's Day edition of the *Sheffield Daily Telegraph* heralded this new era with the headline 'ARMISTICE FOR THE NEW YEAR: FEUD TO END: PEACE CONFERENCE FOR BURYING THE HATCHET'. Needless to say, the long-suffering townsfolk required a little more convincing than a promise from a gangster and a gaudy headline.

To anybody in the know, or who even had the slightest inkling of how Sam Garvin's mind worked, it was painfully obvious that this unexpected truce was nothing more than a mind trick to throw the police of his scent for a while. One would also imagine that Murphy and Winsey were dubious, but could not turn down the offer of being back on the Sky Ring payroll. Yet with the *Telegraph* even comparing the event to the actual armistice of less than a decade before, it is easy to see how many people would be convinced by this facade. It was very much a case of the Sky Ring being ignored, as long as the children were playing happily together. There was even an official statement released, which was anonymous, but was believed to be from the pen of Sam Garvin, which read:

'We feel it is doing no good to any party to indulge in these quarrels. We have heard that the police have stepped in now, determined to stop this sort of thing, and we know that it is the proper time to take the action we have done. We recognise that in the public interest, the attitude of the police is the correct one.'

The mood of goodwill even spread into the courtroom, as the matter of a drunken assault on Thomas Rippon, which had occurred on Christmas night, was still to be addressed. As the guilty parties appeared in the dock on 2 January 1925, Sam Garvin (once again having been guilty of a few festive drinks), Sandy Bowler, and Frank Kidnew were extremely relaxed. Rippon (who had gladly accepted the olive branch since the attack, but had decided not to return to the Sky Ring) failed to attend and testify, and his two ex-gang pals, Murphy and Winsey, swore on oath that the three Park Brigade men had been with them all evening. Mr Morris, defending in the place of Mr Irwin Mitchell (who was presumably taking an extended yuletide holiday) told the magistrate that 'apparently the festive period impregnated the men, and there was a little horse play, but they have settled the differences between themselves'. To which the magistrate responded, 'I hope these men will not make any appearances in this court, this year,' before dismissing the case. As they left the court, Frank Kidnew paused cheerily to wish a Happy New Year to the magistrate.

There were still more serious court proceedings to follow, as the Crown Court appearance of the five men who had attacked Mr and Mrs Dale, and the ex-Mooney men on 8 December were to appear at the Quarter Sessions the next day. The Thomas Rippon assault case had merely been a dress rehearsal for this particular event. Things began well for the Park Brigade, with the victim, Mr Dale, failing to attend court. Murphy and Winsey then appeared, also as the victims, and swore on oath that neither of them even knew who Mr Dale was. However, despite his attempt to sabotage the trial with his men using the story he had instructed them to use, Sam Garvin had failed to take into account the evidence against them.

The prosecution counsel had another trick up their sleeve, despite losing their leading witnesses. They had the testimony of eleven policemen who had turned up at the house that night, including three who had followed the gang for quite some time on that evening. All eleven men swore on oath that the men they had seen attacking the house were Gil Marsh, Ernest Scott, Sandy Bowler, William Carr and William Wareham. The presiding judge was not a regular on the Sheffield legal circuit, and seemed genuinely unaware of the gang situation, and how it had become so out of control. He listened with interest as each police officer gave their statement, and asked many questions along the way. This was unusual, and was rather an unsettling experience for the men in the dock. During one testimony, the judge asked a police officer if it was difficult for the police to keep control over the gangs, to which the constable honestly replied, 'We can rule them if we get assistance from the Bench. They have bound them over at times and have appeared to ridicule the matter.' This was enough for the jury, who unanimously passed a guilty verdict, just hours later.

In summing up before passing sentence, the judge made it clear that the stories he had heard were nothing short of disgraceful, adding that 'adventures of that kind must be stopped'. Gil Marsh, who had attacked Mr Dale with the stool leg was imprisoned for twelve months, Sandy Bowler was sentenced to nine months, Ernest Scott and William Wareham for six months each. William Carr was released without charge.

To say that Sam Garvin was angry was an understatement. Four of his top men had been given the toughest sentences handed out to any of the gang members since the feud began, and the outcome which he had so carefully manufactured was turned on its head. He was especially angry to hear himself named in court by the judge in a speech made to the jury before sentencing commenced:

> 'You have got to ask yourselves whether there was not some person behind all this, whether instructions were given before this case was brought. It is suggested that a man called Samuel Garvin is the deus ex machina. He pulls the strings, and his puppets dance accordingly'

To be so publicly named by the judge had infuriated Garvin, as he felt that not only had he been let down by the defence counsel, he had also been let down by the unconvincing performances of his charges. There had been a lot of work done, and arrangements made, for absolutely nothing.

The days following the court case were especially quiet, as Garvin left the running of the Sky Ring to his men, and retreated to his Park Hill home, where he is said to have brooded over the defeat for quite some time. He was not a man who tolerated defeat, and this particular one would force him to play his hand once again. This was to be another dangerous choice, but one which had to be made, given the grand scheme of things. His right-hand man and main bodyguard, Sandy Bowler, would be staying at His Majesty's pleasure for quite some time, and three other men who were invaluable to the business had joined Bowler for a spot of hard labour. This was a loss that Garvin had not expected. What followed would be a risky piece of business, but one that would at least shore the Park Brigade and their business interests up financially. However, as with everything Sam Garvin did, it came with the threat of serious violence carried out upon his orders, and would make Sheffield a dangerous place to live once more.

The New Year agreement made between the warring factions lasted for less than a month. Things had seemed to be going smoothly, as the Park Brigade and the ex-Mooney men worked together to keep the Sky Ring profitable and protected, all in the absence of the Garvin, who had taken to his home since the farcical trial of his closest allies. However, the whole armistice was to come crashing down on the day that Garvin chose to resurface. This was to be the first meeting of the Sky Ring committee, where the funds would be divided between each party, and future plans for the business discussed. No such talks of this kind were to take place, not on this day, and not on any day.

The former Mooney Gang members must have been suspicious when their new employer arrived at the meeting with a large group of men. They had taken the precaution of bringing with them a man named Tom Armstrong, a member of the infamous Brummagem Boys, who was well known for his brute strength and unrivalled thuggery and had come to stay with his friend, Spud Murphy. Yet, as always, they found themselves outnumbered and outgunned. Garvin wasted no time on social niceties, and bluntly told Murphy, Winsey and Armstrong that they would receive no money and that the Sky Ring was property of the Park Brigade. He accused them of failing in the tasks he had set for them, and told them in no uncertain terms that they were no longer associates of the Park Brigade.

What followed was a heated argument to say the least, with Armstrong especially only restraining himself due to the number of men that Garvin had brought with him. This was a bitter end to a short period of cooperation, and one of the shortest peace agreements ever undertaken. With no other option, the three ousted men took their leave. It was obvious to everyone that violence was just around the corner, but most would have expected to have to wait for more than a matter of minutes before it reared its ugly head. Yet as the three made their way down the steep Park Hill Lane towards the city centre, they suddenly found themselves being chased by around fifty men. This was a coordinated attack, and the mob had clearly been lying in wait for their targets to leave the meeting, angry and dejected. The three figures on the hill were easy targets, and they only had to frighten them in order to complete the task set by their paymaster. It would be the easiest orders they would ever have to follow.

Tom Armstrong must have wondered what he had let himself in for, having only attended the meeting with his friends to ensure that the money was divided up equally, and that nothing untoward would take place. How little he knew of Sam Garvin, and much he must have trusted Spud Murphy to agree to offer his support on this particular occasion. This was a clear message sent by Garvin that their presence in Park Hill would no longer be tolerated, and that in no circumstances should they ever climb this hill again. Under a hail of stones, and with their chasers gaining ground on them, the three managed to make it to the house of a friend, where they managed to barricade themselves safely in until the police arrived.

Having escorted the three men to the safety of West Bar, the police, as well as the three sacrificed pawns, were no longer under any illusion that the armistice had been nothing more than a sham. Garvin had cleverly used the ex-Mooney men and the local newspapers to legitimise his false promises, and was now just as dangerous as he ever had been. Murphy and Winsey had a choice – to leave town, or to prepare themselves for a war that they could never win. Surprisingly, but in keeping with their characters, they did give the option of leaving Sheffield more than a moment's thought. They had grown used to defending themselves, and still had a small amount of business to attend to on the race tracks, where they still held the gambling concessions vacated so abruptly by George Mooney. They were also wise enough to realise that they had never been anything more than unwitting pawns in a game of influence and propaganda, and must have wished that they had not played their respective roles in keeping at least some of the Park Brigade out of prison. However, now was not a time for hindsight, it was a time for survival in the face of a powerful enemy. There would never be another erudite statement to the press from Sam Garvin, explaining the collapse of his much-publicised peace treaty. Things just simply reverted to the way they had been before. The Park Brigade held sole ownership of the Sky Ring, and the ex-cohorts of George Mooney went about their lives quietly and in a constant state of fear.

The city had barely had time to come to terms with the new peaceful gangs before the violence erupted again, so for most of the population of Sheffield, it was as if the warring gangs had never gone away. The same applied to the police, who had enjoyed just three weeks of relative calm within the city. The patrols and no-go areas had never been altered, and the orders from the higher echelons of the police had never changed. The constables had still been briefed to value their own safety, and to call for as much assistance as possible when attending any call out in Park Hill or West Bar. Therefore, it was business as usual for the boys in blue.

With Garvin no doubt looking down of the city from his hilltop office, this was a panoramic view of the city he held solely in his hands once more. Yes, he had broken his word, but there was not a man or gang in that city who could do anything about it. Once again, the former bookmaker held all of the cards.

With the explosive events on Park Hill Lane the talk of the town for days to come, another interesting development in the story had been missed by everyone involved; namely, that Murphy and Winsey were not the only men to have returned to West Bar that week. The Mooney house on Corporation Street had also been repopulated, its owner having returned to his hometown during the brief, but promising, period of peace in the city.

Chapter 7

Rebuilding Bedlam

'The wreckage of stars – I build a world from this wreckage.'

Friedrich Nietzsche, German Philosopher (1844–1900)

The *Sheffield Mail* had, once again, been the voice of reality amongst the city's more exuberant press. Unlike the *Telegraph*, the *Mail* had not been cleverly conned into promoting the propaganda of Sam Garvin. Instead, the critical tone of their observations on the gangs, the judiciary, and the resources available to the police, was to continue into this new year. Without having resorted to over-sentimental headlines in response to a peace treaty which would never last, the *Mail* had simply kept its powder dry during the few weeks of relative calm, allowing its reporters to be fully armed when the armistice came crashing down. There was to be no self-congratulatory pomp in their accurate foresight, just a reprisal of the stance which the newspaper had taken against the gangs during the previous years.

Rather than breaking the news of the disingenuous collapse of the peace agreement with a 'told-you-so' headline, the *Mail* simply resumed its normal agenda, leading the 23 January edition with 'FIRM HAND NEEDED FOR THE SHEFFIELD GANGS', a sentiment which had long been adopted by the paper, its readers, and the police who found common ground with the respected publication. So good was the relationship between the *Mail* and the police, that Chief Constable John Hall-Dalwood had once again agreed to share his opinions with his preferred publication, giving an honest and damning interview on the ability of the police to deal with the problem in hand:

> 'We have broken the Rings up, we have made multiple raids and brought the men before the magistrates, and we, as police, can do nothing more. So far as the hooliganism is concerned, it must be well known to everybody who reads the papers that we are bringing men in sometimes three of four times a week for these offences.

Whenever the law is broken we bring men before the magistrates.
We are handicapped by the fact that the prosecutors are sometimes
'got at', and we cannot bring our witnesses, but we do everything
in our power.'

The *Mail*, in its contribution to the feature, wholeheartedly agreed, citing
an occasion where a number of men were arrested whilst in the process
of illegal gambling, only to be taken before the magistrate and fined forty
shillings each. The minute the proceedings had ended, a number of taxis
were summoned, with the express purpose of returning the gamblers to the
Sky Ring. Adding that the police were 'very discouraged' by the attitude
of the judiciary, the *Mail* also branded the sentences handed out to the
gang members over the last two years as 'miserably inadequate'. Again, the
magistrates had been openly criticised by the protectors of the people, and
the voice of the people.

This was shown to be depressingly accurate within the next few days, as
two of the highest-ranking men still at liberty with the Park Brigade were
to appear in court charged with threatening to kill the steward of a local
club, the Victoria on Sycamore Street. Arthur Whitham and George Ganner
Wheywell were the men in the dock on this occasion. The prosecution had
gone to great lengths to tell the tale of how the two men arrived late at the
venue, only to be told by the steward that they would not be allowed in at this
late hour. Reportedly, Wheywell had used the old chestnut, 'Do you know
who I am?' before Whitham threatened to return with a revolver, warning
the steward that 'his card (was) marked'.

The magistrate, William Clegg, who had led an interesting life, having
played football for Sheffield Wednesday and England, and had also defended
the infamous Charlie Peace during his former role as a solicitor, seemed
almost bored with the trial taking place before him, and hurried the case
along, before binding Wheywell and Whitham over in the sums of £25 and
£10 respectively.

On printing their take on the outcome of this trial, the *Mail* was inundated
by letters from concerned members of the public. Keen to cement their place
as the voice of the people, a large selection of the letters were published
the very next day, alongside a public challenge to the judiciary to explain
their reluctance in levying fitting punishments upon the troublesome gang
members. Unsurprisingly, no official response was ever received from either
the magistrates or the Watch Committee. Both parties had circled their
wagons effectively, and would refuse to make any comment on the obvious

lack of action. The *Mail* could not directly accuse any of these men of being in the pay of Sam Garvin, but was more than happy to publish the letters of those who did so. Knowing full well that to take action against these 'libellous' letters would mean a public legal case, in which the matter would require full and public discussion, was enough to deter the parties involved from filing a grievance, which would perhaps provide further proof of some very dubious goings-on in the business end of the courtrooms.

However, events which would soon occur would bring the focus very back onto the gangs and their criminal activities, which would, in turn, focus the spotlight back onto the reluctant magistrates. Sheffield was about to see a second wave of violence, and the return of some unwanted, and unexpected, alliances.

By mid-February 1925, a mere six weeks since the fictitious peace agreement, the inter-gang assaults had once again begun in earnest, and it would seem that Sam Garvin had, on this occasion, been willing to get his hands dirty in the name of opening up old wounds, along with the assistance of two very close cohorts.

During the eventful meeting at the Sky Ring, in which the short-lived partnership between the two factions was unceremoniously dissolved, Ernest Chapman was very much the one who got away, having failed to attend, and therefore not being part of the small group of men running for their lives from a stone-pelting mob. If anything, Chapman was more of a thorn in the side of Sam Garvin than any of the three men who had been chased from Sky Edge that day. He had once been a leading member of the Park Brigade, having even taken part in the infamous storming of the Mooney home in 1923. However, he had since found common ground with Spud Murphy and Peter Winsey, and had chosen to be part of their ex-Mooney Gang ventures, rather than remain at the service of Garvin.

During the few weeks that the treaty was in place, this had not been an obvious issue, but the subsequent reneging of this agreement left Chapman in a very dangerous situation. He was cast out of the Park Brigade, and would be forced to seek cover with the men whose company he had come to prefer. Having led a quiet life indoors since then, Chapman had decided on a rare outing to a pub with his friend 'Cosh' Burns (who, unsurprisingly, was also an ex-gang member). Yet, the two couldn't have made a more unfortunate choice of venue, as, arriving in the Barleycorn Hotel; the two friends were greeted with the sight of Sam Garvin, casually leaning at the bar.

Without acknowledging Garvin, and hoping that the past would be left alone, the two men approached the bar and ordered two pints of bitter. However, without making eye contact with Chapman and Burns, Garvin turned to the landlord and said, 'Don't serve these two, they are traitors to me.'

It must have been a heart-stopping moment for Ernest Chapman as he witnessed his friend turn on his heels and march up to Garvin. 'How long have you been the landlord here, Garvin?' was the response. The actual landlord then interjected, asking Chapman and Burns to leave, as he didn't want any trouble in his establishment. A moment of intense eye contact followed between Burns and Garvin, who had now been joined by two fellow Park men, his brother Bob, and a man named George Butler. Noticing the backup, Burns headed for the door, quickly followed by Chapman, who didn't make it out of the pub in time to avoid the consequences.

Garvin had no interest in 'Cosh' Burns, he was nothing more than a thug for hire, but Ernest Chapman, had double-crossed him, and the whole of the Park Brigade. Unable to contain his rage any longer, Garvin stalked towards the door, and spun the retreating Chapman around as he was about to exit. A blow was struck by Garvin, reportedly with something held in his hand, ironically, most likely a cosh. Standing over his fallen opponent, he growled over his shoulder to the two men who had come to offer support – 'Kill him'. At this, Butler swung an almighty punch to the face of the stricken Chapman, which was followed up by a brutal and cowardly kick by Bob Garvin to the face of the prostrate Chapman.

The bravado of Burns had deserted him before Chapman had even hit the ground, and he took flight up the street as quickly as his legs could carry him. Luckily for Chapman, his cohort wasn't quite as useless as it seemed, as he at least managed to alert a nearby policeman to the trouble in the Barleycorn Hotel. By the time he had called for assistance, and arrived at the bar, the policeman was greeted with an empty pub, save for Chapman unconscious and bleeding in the doorway. Regaining his senses a little later, Chapman, who had nothing left to lose, had no hesitation in naming his attackers, who were rounded up and arrested that evening.

Appearing in court the next day, the three men, who had been charged with assault, had decided to leave the talking to Mr J.W. Fenoughty, Sam Garvin's long time solicitor. Chapman appeared as a witness, bandaged and bruised, but Burns had thought better of it, and had taken this opportunity to walk away from the trouble he had caused for his friend.

Chapman was reminded by Fenoughty, that he had, in fact, once been in the very same dock with Sam Garvin, who had then paid his surety after the Mooney home attack. Having been forced to admit this was the case, Chapman then went on to describe how his ties with the Park brigade had recently been severed forever. As always, Fenoughty was keen to avoid this case being labelled as a 'gang' crime, and addressed the magistrate, saying 'if two boys have a fight in Meersbrook (Park), it's a gang. Let us have fairness and common sense when dealing with ordinary cases of assault.'

As it would turn out, the magistrate was more than fair with the three men in the dock, and completely dismissed the case against them. His reasoning was that Burns had not been sufficiently affected by the incident to testify, and Chapman and Garvin had long endured a difficult relationship, which was always likely to end in this manner. It was no surprise to anyone that Sam Garvin had managed to walk free from court. However, the complete lack of any kind of punishment was viewed with a wide sense of suspicion. Fenoughty had performed his job admirably, and it would seem that the magistrate had also followed the script to the letter.

It is worth mentioning at this point, that a young member of the Park Brigade appeared as a witness for the defence in this case. Wilfred Fowler, who would soon be just as infamous as his employer, if not more so, had finally been charged with carrying out an important duty, one which he performed admirably.

As always, the trial of one or more gang members had brought with it a large crowd of onlookers, mostly other members of gang who had come to offer moral support to their unfortunate friends. This occasion was no different, and the court was experiencing a lot of visitors, both on the inside and the outside. In keeping with recent trials, those on the outside were much less friendly than those in the public gallery. But, on this occasion, there was a man present who has yet to appear in this book, but played one of the most important roles of any of the gang members. His name was George Newbould, and fate had cast him in the role of kingmaker.

Newbould had begun his short gang career just few months before, having been a friend of Peter Winsey. He had long been regarded as a dangerous and almost psychotic man, but had never sworn any allegiance to either side of the Sheffield divide. In fact, he had originally been thrown into the melting pot as a victim of gang violence. As an occasional associate of the Mooney gang, and outspoken in his criticism of the Garvin regime, Newbould was always going to find himself in trouble since the collapse of

George Mooneys's empire. It was, therefore, no real surprise when he found himself on the wrong side of Sam Garvin at the latter end of Christmas Day, when the two ended up drinking in the same pub.

Knowing that Newbould was not recognised as a gang member, Garvin had quickly realised that he could find himself in serious trouble for what happened next. Along with Frank Kidnew, Sandy Barlow and William Wareham, Garvin had immediately laid into Newbould verbally, and as the neutral hard man was never one to back down, a fight soon ensued, seeing Newbould being severely beaten as he tried to solely defend himself against three attackers. As the foggy heads awoke the next morning, Garvin realised that he was in a bit of a bind. He had attacked a non-gang member in public, with three other men against one. Newbould was also brave enough to see his attackers answer for the assault in court. This left no option other than for Garvin to appeal to Newbould with the one thing he could offer; power. Now follows the real plan behind the New Year treaty.

Newbould, although officially a private citizen, was something of a mentor to the remaining Mooney men after the midnight flit of their former leader. He was older than the others, and had a seriously frightening reputation. His reason for never officially joining a gang was that, he had never needed to. People just didn't cross George Newbould. Yet, as the younger men went about their business without guidance and support, Newbould soon realised that he could easily take control of the former Mooney Gang, if only there were a gang to take over. The power he now held in his hands over Sam Garvin could change everything, but only if a deal could be made.

The attendees at the infamous New Year meeting were never revealed, but it did come to light that Newbould was definitely in attendance, and was the man who brokered the deal in which part of the running of the Sky Ring would be placed back into the hands of the former Mooney Gang, with himself receiving a good share of the profits. In return, Garvin had required a signed document from Newbould, which cleared the Park Brigade boss of any crime committed against him. It was also understood that the former Mooney men would come to the aid of his men in court, and make sure that none of his top cohorts would find themselves imprisoned. This had all worked swimmingly until the judge decided to continue the case against Garvin's closest allies, even without witnesses for the prosecution. This, unfortunately, had been the catalyst behind the early collapse of the treaty, as Garvin realised that he no longer required the assistance of his former enemies.

With the aid of Newbould, Garvin had briefly become the man who held the city solely in his palm, and was free to act as he pleased, knowing that what little remnants of an opposition remained, would be swiftly deterred by their new mentor should any trouble occur. Newbould had secured the crown for Garvin, but only for a short period of time. Upon the imprisonment of his four closest friends, and his most valued comrades in arms, Garvin had quickly realised that there was nothing left for him in regards to the current deal. He had the safety guaranteed by Newbould's signed statement, and had lost his friends to the prison system despite the best efforts of all involved. He simply no longer had a use for his former opponent. As such, Garvin could easily welsh on his previous promises, safe in the knowledge that the only repercussion would be a few angry men, but nowhere near enough to cause any serious issues for his gang. No longer would he need to lose his valuable profits to those who had had their chance at running the Sky Ring, and had lost it at the merest sign of trouble.

However, in thinking that he would be faced with only a few lone stragglers, Garvin had been a little naive. Newbould was a man who commanded a great deal of respect, and along with the former Mooney Gang members, he was more than capable of raising an army, but it was never expected that he could raise one large enough to disturb the balance of power.

As the trial of the Garvin brothers and George Butler ended in the knowledge that there was to be no punishment delivered on this occasion, those who had inhabited the dock and the public gallery began to trickle out onto Castle Street. Cigarettes were passed around and lit, and conversation was of a cheerful nature. Yet something was amiss. A good-sized crowd had gathered on the opposite side of the road, all men, all serious looking, and all staring at the large group leaving the courthouse. A lot of the faces were familiar, and some of them were even more than familiar, they were faces of enemies and friends from the past.

The sternest looking of the men was somebody who had a serious bone to pick with Sam Garvin – George Newbould. Flanking him were the usual suspects, Spud Muphy and Peter Winsey. These were also men with a grudge, and men who could prove to be dangerous with the right amount of back-up. Tom Armstrong was still on the scene, his huge figure towering over the usually impressive Newbould, as he stood behind him with eyes trained on the scene on the opposite side of the road. It would seem that his secondment from the Brummagem Boys had been extended, and he was now residing in the spare bedroom of the Newbould residence. However, it was two of the men a little further down the line that caused the most consternation. Firstly, it would appear that Albert Foster had returned from exile, and was looking to avenge the brutal attack that had seen him forced to leave the city and take refuge in the equally dangerous streets of Birmingham.

Finally, the presence of another man seemed almost surreal to those who warily watched from the other side of the street. Tucked in amongst the stern looking crowd was George Ganner Wheywell, who had secretly defected to the newly formed army, and was casting his steely gaze at one man in particular; Sam Garvin. The man whose assault had been the reason for this trial was also a defector from the Park Brigade. Ernest Chapman would appear to have been instrumental in convincing his friend to change allegiance, and the man who had just lost out in court was to be the eventual winner, as he left the court and crossed the street to join his reception party.

The police who were tasked to patrol the court had immediately called for back-up, which quickly arrived from both the Central police station, and the West Bar station. Forming a protective line along the road between the two groups, the assembled constables shouted at the two groups to leave the area in separate directions. With reluctance, the groups eventually dispersed. This was not the time to settle scores, not with so many of Sheffield's finest around. It was a time for a show of force, and a warning that Garvin had not killed off his rivals just yet. The Park Brigade had the numbers, but the new mob undoubtedly had the edge when it came to muscle.

This stand-off had forced Garvin's hand somewhat; he had the choice of either remaining calm and rethinking his current position, or striking out at the mob that had publicly sought to intimidate him as he left the court. Unusually for Garvin, he opted for the less sensible of the two options, and decided to strike at the very heart of the newly formed enemy.

On 1 March, Newbould had been disturbed by a knock on his door during the evening, and had opened it to find a man named John Towler on his doorstep. Towler was a fairly innocuous member of the Park Brigade, and, although being recognised by Newbould, did a superb job of keeping a cheery and friendly tone whilst asking if Tom Armstrong was at home. Newbould, who, perhaps naively, told Towler that Armstrong had gone out for the evening was then surprised to see the cheery expression of his evening caller change, and as his visitor simply uttered 'good', saw the bottle that crashed into his skull too late to move out of the way. Newbould had been felled, and his bodyguard was away drinking in some part of the city. Towler and the two accomplices who had stood pressed against the walls at either side of the door made their getaway. Newbould was treated in hospital for a severe head wound, which required a number of stitches, and was consigned to bed for almost a week with an almighty concussion. However, he had been well enough to name Towler to the police who visited his hospital bedside.

After a short trial, in which Towler, bizarrely, opted to represent himself, the defendant come defence counsel ended up being on the end of a custodial sentence. He had done himself no favours by conducting his own defence, and had walked straight into several traps set by Mr S. Grant, prosecuting. He was sentenced to four months in the Second Division, a prison sentence without hard labour.

The inevitable retribution, organised by Newbould from his sick bed occurred just two days later and was little more than a more brutal variation of the attack which had left the de facto leader of the new gang stitched up and concussed. This was a deliberate warning that anything Garvin could do, Newbould could repay with interest. The victim of the revenge attack was George Butler, who had become a trusted ally of Garvin since the imprisonment of his right-hand man, Sandy Bowler. The location of the attack was also deliberately planned, as it took place right outside a boxing event organised and hosted by Garvin himself.

George Butler had been inside the venue on Edmund Road for some time, but had eventually stepped outside to have a chat with an old friend without the din of the boxing match. His assailants had been waiting patiently in a nearby alleyway for this moment and without warning, emerged from the shadows. Butler was instantly felled by a vicious blow to the head and did not regain consciousness for a number of days. However, his friend had seen the attack take place, and described to the police the sight of Albert Foster brandishing an iron bar, and Ganner Wheywell holding a metal fish mallet. It was Foster who had inflicted the blow so vicious that Wheywell and his mallet had proved to be surplus to requirements on this occasion.

For ten days, Butler was at death's door. He had suffered a depressed fracture of the skull, and the prognosis was that he was unlikely to ever recover. Knowing the damage he had done, Foster once again fled the city, heading back to Birmingham where he would be harboured by the Brummagem Boys for a second time.

It was over a month before he was eventually apprehended in a nationwide manhunt. He was hauled before the Sheffield magistrates for a pre-trial hearing, but given that his victim was still unable to leave hospital, the case was adjourned, and Foster was remanded in custody until the trial could take place. As usual the witness to the assault had gone missing, and only the word of Butler was available for the prosecution counsel to work with. The trial was once again adjourned, but Foster, no doubt expecting to be granted bail, was immediately imprisoned for three months on a charge he seemed to have forgotten all about; the arrears in maintenance owed to his ex-wife. When the case had been rearranged, and the witness finally located. Foster was taken from his cell to answer the charges of Grievous Bodily Harm against George Butler. The seriousness of the offence meant that a further custodial sentence was inevitable, and Foster was lucky only to receive a further 18 months of hard labour.

During Butler's time in prison, the gang war in the city had escalated back to its former levels, with both groups having recruited a number of junior members. This mean that those who had previously held junior roles were now on their way to becoming serious gang men, some of whom would play a major part in the events which were to unfold in the aftermath of this new war being declared.

Chapter 8

The Fall of a Mighty Oak

'Everything that happens before death is what counts.'

Ray Bradbury, American Author (1920–2012)

I f you were to visit the barracks at Hillsborough today, you would no doubt be a little underwhelmed at the development of the site. Some of the original features are still present, but you would find most over the compound dominated by a giant Morrison's supermarket, and a Poundland looking down on where the parade ground (now a huge car park) would have been. The Garrison Hotel, which stands proudly and with an air of superiority over the McDonalds behind it, still holds onto the beautiful architecture and original features of the Barracks, but is the one shining light in what has become a corporate mess, with clumsy attempts made to match the newer features to the original buildings. Whatever its current state, the Barracks compound has an important place in Sheffield's history. Originally built in 1848, the War Department and later the Ministry of Defence used the site to train and house troops for over eighty years. It was, at one time, one of the best military bases in the country, and had been purpose built to provide everything an army could need.

In its heyday, the site boasted a huge area dedicated to the soldiers' dormitories, an impressive mess, quarters for over forty officers, and also its own chapel. Alongside these facilities were a sixty bed hospital, a dental clinic, and enough stable area to house over 200 horses. For those who misbehaved during their army career, there were also a guard room, a police room, and several detention cells. This wasn't just a home for squaddies on basic training; this was a full-scale army facility. Families were well catered for, with fifty married quarters, a school, and a Polo field and riding school. The Barracks was nothing short of a small town, situated right in the middle of a heavily populated area within a large city. The busiest time for the Barracks was always when the threat of war was in the air, and many army units were brought to Sheffield before and during the Boer War to hone their skills before undertaking the long and difficult journey to South Africa.

The main residents of the compound during this time were the Yorkshire Dragoons and the Yorkshire Hussars, both of which were well respected and highly decorated regiments. Also having trained at the Barracks were the Royal Horse Artillery, and the Royal Irish Rifles. All in all, hundreds of thousands of men, women and children had used the Barracks as a temporary home. However, as time went on, and the act of war began to take on an industrial and mechanical turn, the Barracks became outdated. The mounted regiments had started to be disbanded, or had been transformed into tank or artillery regiments. As such, the compound was sparsely used after the turn of the century. Despite its change in fortune, the place of the giant military facility was cemented in the history of Sheffield. This had been a place which had seen more than its fair share of heroes, and had also seen more than its fair share of casualties being nursed to health. It was, and still is, a monument to those who served the nation, and despite its current use, still cuts an impressive figure in the centre of Hillsborough.

Ironically, the story of one former resident of the Barracks, who tragically died a brave and noble death, is not connected to any real war or genuine military conflict. It is the story of a man who stood up to a dangerous enemy, refusing to be intimidated, and was cut down in his prime as a result of his integrity.

William Francis Plommer was a 34-year-old labourer employed by the Bessemer Company, one of Sheffield's main employers during the boom in industry enjoyed by the city. Although physically impressive, Plommer was known as a kind and gentle man, who had dedicated his life to his country, his work, and his family. He was born in Glasgow, and had been a career soldier since his late teens. The move south to Sheffield had been a happy time for Plommer, as he had met his wife whilst stationed at the Hillsborough Barracks. Keen to start a family and ready to embrace life on Civvy Street, Plommer had left the army in 1912 in order to forge a safe, domestic life for himself and his bride.

However, as the world was plunged into war just two years later, Plommer felt it was his duty to answer the King's call, and re-enlisted. He was to spend the whole of the war serving in the trenches, and saw a large amount of action during his time in France and Belgium. He had reached the rank of sergeant by the end of the war, but was keen to return to the life he had begun to build with the wife he had missed so much during his long and arduous campaign. Returning home, Plommer found himself to be in need of gainful employment, and had already turned down the advances of George Mooney, who was keen to secure the services of such a brave and physically domineering fighting man, when he eventually managed to secure himself a position with the Bessemer Company. The offer to join Mooney must have been tempting, as the money on offer was far more than he would earn as a labourer in the steelworks. Yet Plommer knew that the gang life was not for him, he lacked something which was a basic requirement of any gang member; namely, a sense of malice. To him, violence was for the battlefield, not for the streets of his adopted home.

He was a hard worker, a good husband and father, and a loyal friend. Nobody who knew 'Jock' Plommer had a bad word to say about him. Unfortunately for the former soldier and his young family, he unwittingly became part of another war, but one that lacked honour, courage and legitimacy.

The events which were to lead to his downfall were not of his making, and were a tawdry affair compared with the real battles in which he had found himself during his long and distinguished military career. He deserved a long and happy life, but this was denied him by a moment of madness, and an event which would disgust the majority of his adopted city. It all came about as Plommer stood up for his principles, and had the steely nerve to stare the threat of gang violence stoically in the eye. Jock was a man acting on behalf of a city which had simply had enough of the violence, and had no hesitation in facing the real and terrifying threat that his show of selfless bravery had incurred.

What follows is a story unbefitting a man like Jock Plommer. He deserved a long and happy life, and a noble and gentle death, but was denied both by the criminal element of the city known as 'Little Chicago'. Yet, it is this particular story on which the future of the Sheffield Gangs was eventually decided, and for that at least, the city owes him a great amount of gratitude.

The first seeds of doom were sown on the night before Plommer's untimely death, as he had been unlucky enough to be called upon by a friend in danger. Until now, the former soldier had been enjoying a quiet evening with his family, but the unexpected knock at the door began a chain of events so unfortunate, that Plommer could never have imagined the danger he was placing himself in. The friend in need, Harold Liversidge, had been drinking in the Windsor Hotel, just a stone's throw from the Plommer home. Liversidge, it has to be said, was something of a crook, and was known to many of the gang members, none of whom would have trusted him as far as they could have thrown him.

Yet, on this occasion, he had merely gone for a quiet drink and a game of cards. Exactly what occurred in the Windsor Hotel that evening has never been ascertained, but it would seem that Liversidge had fallen foul of some of his fellow drinkers on this occasion. Unfortunately for him, and ultimately Jock Plommer, these were exactly the kind of men who one would not wish to get into an argument with. At around 10 o'clock, Liversidge went to stand in the street, taking in a little fresh air, when another man followed him out of the busy bar. The man darted towards Liversidge, who was looking the other way with his hands nonchalantly in his pockets, and shouted 'I will make you remember Fowler' before landing a mighty punch in the face of the unexpecting Liversidge.

After coming to his senses Liversidge was all too aware that he was a fair distance from his home, and that there were a number of other men inside the pub who had been drinking with his attacker. Left with two options, returning home and hoping to avoid a further attack on the way, or facing his attacker with his own back-up, he chose the more foolish of the two options, and unwittingly drew a close friend into the firing line.

Plommer lived in the next street to the Windsor Hotel, and was surprised to see his friend panting and nervous on his doorstep. Having explained his predicament, Liversidge pleaded with his pal to join him in returning to the Windsor, if only to ensure that he was not set upon by the attacker's cohorts when challenging him to a fight. Jock could have refused, and gone back to his cosy evening, but he was a man of principle, and was all too happy to fulfil his friend's request. He would go to the pub, but only to ensure that the challenge thrown down by Liversidge was accepted and carried out in a gentlemanly way. This error of judgement would be the decision that sparked a tragic event.

Liversidge and his trusty aide soon located Wilfred Spinks Fowler, who was still drinking in the Windsor Hotel with his older brother, Lawrence, and a group of other men. When confronting his attacker, Liversidge found that only Lawrence Fowler seemed to be interested in coming to his brother's defence as the other men slid away into the snug. Plommer had this effect on people; he was a man that most people liked and respected, and there were very few people who would be foolish enough to challenge him. The older Fowler brother was also reluctant, and was easily subdued by Plommer, who assured him that he was only there to guarantee a fair fight between the two other men. Without the element of surprise, Wilfred Fowler was nowhere near as dangerous. He was younger and more slightly built that Liversidge. However, he had been challenged in front of his brother and his friends, which left the younger Fowler brother no choice but to resume his feud with Liversidge, but this time it would be face to face, and Liversidge would be ready.

To the disappointment of the drinkers who spilled out of the pub to watch, the fight was over very quickly. In a nutshell, Liversidge had knocked ten bells out of Fowler while his older brother was forced to watch, unable to assist due to the heavy hand of Jock Plommer on his shoulder. This had been a very brief spectacle, but one that would lead to terrible consequences.

The next day, while Wilfred Fowler tended his injuries and tried to piece his pride back together, all had been forgotten in the Plommer household. Not one to dwell on this kind of nasty incident, Jock had gone to work at the Bessemer Company as usual, and returned home early in the evening to enjoy dinner with his wife and four young children.

The day had not been so tranquil at the Sky Ring, where Lawrence Fowler had arrived full of rage due to the previous night's events. Meeting with Sam Garvin, he told the tale of how Liversidge had given his brother a sound beating and that he had been prevented from intervening by the threat of Jock Plommer; a man known to Garvin as somebody who had turned down his offer of employment in the not so distant past. Garvin was furious to hear of the incident; yet his rage was not aimed at Harold Liversidge. The public defeat of one of his up and coming gang members was an embarrassment to his organisation; and the reluctance of Lawrence Fowler to make even a failed effort to tip the scales was nothing more than cowardice. As such, Garvin decided that something must be done to address the situation. He would organise a mob to descend upon Attercliffe that evening, and, whether they liked it or not, the Fowler brothers were to regain their honour in front of those that had seen them capitulate so easily the night before.

There was also something of an ulterior motive in Garvin's plan. He was aware that two of the newly united rival gang also lived in the vicinity, and would take the opportunity to kill three birds with one stone. With this in mind, the gang he organised was large, and consisted of several of his most trusted men. The importance of this revenge attack was so great that, on this occasion, Garvin would not trust his men to take care of matters on his behalf, and told Lawrence Fowler in no uncertain terms that he would

The Sheffield Pals Battalion band posing for a photograph in Norfolk Park before being transported to their training depot.
Courtesy of wartimememoriesproject.com

Modern day Corporation Street, the area where George Mooney would live for most of his early life. *Courtesy of mapio.net*

John William Streets, Sheffield's much under-appreciated First World War poet.

Courtesy of warpoets.org.uk

A census document showing George Mooney and his family living in Corporation Street. Mooney was 10 years old at the time. *Courtesy of sheffieldhistory.co.uk*

The West Bar area of Sheffield in 1920, where the majority of the Mooney Gang lived. *Courtesy of pinterest.com*

A Photograph of some of the Mooney Gang members. George Mooney appears on the far right, and 'Spud' Murphy on the far left. *Courtesy of picturesheffield.com*

A photograph depicting a typical northern police regiment in 1920. *Courtesy of flickr.com*

Samuel Garvin, leader of the Park Brigade, and feared gangster. *Courtesy of The Sheffield Gang Wars by J.P Bean*

A modern day photograph of the steep road leading to the Sky Ring, where the 'pikers' would be stationed to keep an eye out for police and rival gangs. *Courtesy of peterwynmosey.com*

The view of the city from Sky Edge, home of the infamous Sky Ring. *Courtesy of peterwynmosey.com*

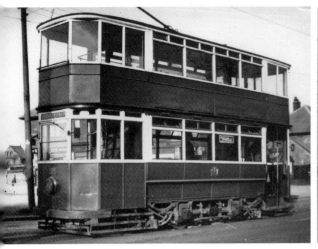

A 1920's Sheffield tram, often used by gang members to make a quick getaway.
Courtesy of sheffieldhistory.co.uk

A 1920's solid wheeled bus, similar to that in which the police raided the Sky Ring.
Courtesy of londonbusmuseum.com

William 'Jock' Plommer (left), and his alleged killers, Wilfred Fowler (centre) and Lawrence Folwer (right).
Courtesy of pressreader.com

A postcard showing the Bessemer Company where William 'Jock' Plommer worked as a labourer after leaving the army. *Courtesy of flickr.com*

Sheffield Royal Infirmary, where William 'Jock' Plommer was taken, but died of his wounds. *Courtesy of sth.nhs.uk*

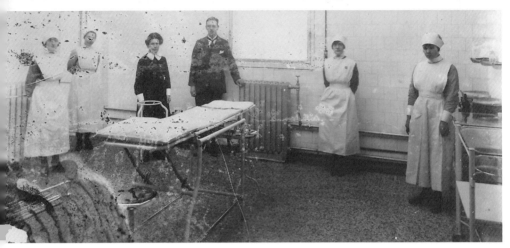

A 1920 hospital operation theatre. Many gang members would have been stitched back together in such an environment. *Courtesy of hhtandn.org*

The exact location of William 'Jock' Plommer's murder. The assault took place by the street lamp on the corner. *Courtesy of the author*

An artist's depiction of the area of Attercliffe where William 'Jock' Plommer lived and died. Painted by George Cunningham. *Courtesy of ourbroomhall.org.uk*

A modern day view of Princess Street, where the Plommer home would have been before the area was developed. *Courtesy of the author*

Burngreave Cemetery Chapel, where thousands of people would say farewell to the deceased William 'Jock' Plommer. *Courtesy of the author*

Burngreave Cemetery, where William 'Jock' Plommer was laid to rest. *Courtesy of the author*

A short bayonet similar to the suspected murder weapon, which was never found. *Courtesy of new.liveauctioneers.com*

mos Stewart, sentenced to
en year penal servitude for the
nanslaughter of William 'Jock'
lommer. *Courtesy of thestar.co.uk*

Bob Garvin, brother of Sam
Garvin. Acquitted for the
manslaughter of William
'Jock' Plommer, but
imprisoned for an assault
on Harry Rippon. *Courtesy of thestar.co.uk*

George Wills, sentenced
to ten year penal servitude
for the manslaughter of
William 'Jock' Plommer.
Courtesy of thestar.co.uk

Stevenson Road, Darnall. The remains of the housing which was home to Wilfred Fowler and
his family, with lodger Fred Goddard. *Courtesy of picturesheffield.com*

The entrance to Ardmore Street, Darnall. Home to Lawrence Fowler and his family before
demolition. *Courtesy of picturesheffield.com*

Sgt William
Robinson, the leader
of the notorious
Flying Squad.
*Courtesy of The Sheffield
Gang Wars by J.P Bean*

PC Walter Loxley, the
only existing photograph
of this feared member of
the Flying Squad.
*Courtesy of The Sheffield Gang
Wars by J.P Bean*

Sir Percy Sillitoe, the man who changed
the face of law and order in Sheffield.
He would later go on to do the same in
Glasgow, and would eventually become
head of MI5. *Courtesy of gettyimages.co.uk*

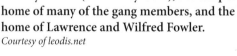

Armley Prison (or Armley Gaol), the temporary
home of many of the gang members, and the last
home of Lawrence and Wilfred Fowler.
Courtesy of leodis.net

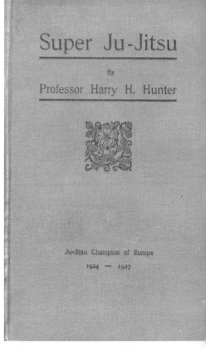

The book on Ju Jitsu written by
Professor Harry Hunter, the man who
was to train the Sheffield police in
martial arts. *Courtesy of ebay.com*

be overseeing the proceedings, and did not expect to be embarrassed or disappointed any further.

Wilfred Fowler had been hastily patched up for the evening, and was no doubt disappointed that Harold Liversidge was not to be the target of the attack. Garvin had conceded that his man had been beaten in a fair fight, and had no desire to repay the favour. The main focus of the evening was to seek revenge against the man who had stood in the way of his gang, and forced members of the Park Brigade to be defeated. In the back of Garvin's mind was also the planned assault on the two gang men, Arthur Whitton and Harry Rippon (brother of Thomas Rippon), who were known to be close friends of Jock Plommer. Which led to the question, had Plommer acted merely out of honour? Or were his actions due to some kind of affiliation with the newly formed gang?

It would later be confirmed that Jock Plommer had no such ties to the gang, and had ensured a fair fight between Harold Liversidge and Wilfred Fowler out of his own sense of fair play and honour. However, as things would turn out, this fact would be very much irrelevant, as it would end up as nothing more than a footnote to a horrific tale.

As night fell, and Jock Plommer finished his family dinner, the quiet calm of Attercliffe was punctured by a number of voices shouting in the street. Garvin's posse had arrived; and had immediately taken to loitering in Princess Street outside the Plommer family home, from where they called into the night sky for Jock to come out and face them. Unlike George Mooney, Plommer's first reaction was not to hide away and put his family at risk of attack; it was to go out into the street and put a stop to the fracas before it went any further. He would have been only too aware of the 'home visits' paid by gang members, and as such, told his wife that he was going outside to talk some sense into these unwelcome visitors.

Striding out of 42, Princess Street, like man without a care in the world, Plommer did not falter as he saw the gang assembled in the street. Having calmly asked what the commotion was about, and receiving a volley of abuse in return, it was not long before Jock Plommer realised that he would have to raise his fists on this occasion. In a fair fist fight, Plommer would have beaten almost any man in the city, but the Park Brigade had decided that there had been enough fair play on the previous evening, and had come prepared for battle. His attackers had been under no illusion that they would use their fists against such a strong man, and as they drew closer to their prey, a number of weapons were drawn.

What followed was a blur of limbs and fierce blows. Plommer had managed to inflict some damage of his own on the first couple of assailants, but stood little chance as all eight gang members descended upon him. Yet, he did not fall, and had almost made it back to his front door when one of the men picked up a small scooter belonging to Plommer's 4-year-old son, and felled him with a mighty blow to the back of the head. But as it would turn out, this knockout blow was nothing more than a coup de grace; the real damage had been done during the melee. Garvin called his men off, and instructed them to make a quick getaway. There was still work to be done on this particular evening, and they were to regroup later to continue their mission.

However, the getaway was not as stealthy as would have been hoped, and a police constable noticed a group of men running away from Princess Street. PC Daniel Hogan was too far behind to catch up with the five suspicious characters, but did not have to travel far to find the remaining three. The Fowler brothers, along with George Wills, were sitting nonchalantly on the kerb outside a chip shop. All three seemed out of breath and buoyed by some kind of victory, this combined with the state of Wilfred Fowler following his previous beating immediately rang alarm bells with the young constable, who was about to start questioning the three loitering men, but was interrupted by screams from further down the road. The screams had come from Plommer's wife, who knelt by the prostrate body of her husband. PC Hogan rushed towards the screams, and was greeted by the sight of Jock Plommer, face down on the ground and lying in an ever-increasing pool of blood. His head had been cut open by the blow from the scooter, but more seriously, two stab wounds oozed copious amounts of blood from his stomach and left side. An ambulance was sent for, and having called for assistance, PC Hogan was now able to ask the hysterical Mrs Plommer what had happened. She was able to confirm that her husband had gone outside to confront a group of men, but was unable to identify any of them. As such, the sight of the three men outside the chip shop had slipped from the mind of the young constable.

A quick search of the crime scene unearthed some brutal paraphernalia. Thrown into hedges and gutters were a number of weapons, including razors, an iron chain, and several pokers. However, the object which had been used to stab Jock Plommer was not found, although was suspected by detectives to be a bayonet. In the meantime, the stricken Jock Plommer had been taken by ambulance to the nearby Royal Infirmary, but had been unable to fight back against his multiple injuries. He was declared dead upon arrival at the hospital, and the police were now investigating a murder.

Unaware of the condition of their earlier victim, the remaining members of the gang had regrouped as per Garvin's orders. The Fowler brothers and George Wills had not joined them, but the decision was made to go ahead without them. The men who remained were more than capable of handling their intended victim. Harry Rippon was extremely unlucky to run into his attackers that night. The gang members had been searching for him for quite some time before they would eventually find their prey. In fact, the Bull and Oak pub had been the last place on their list, and they had stopped for a drink before setting out on their journey home after a seemingly fruitless mission.

Known locally for his impressive baritone singing voice, Rippon often liked to go on something of a pub crawl, where he would sing for his drinks at each pub on the way. On this occasion, the Bull and Oak would also be his last stop before returning home, which makes what happened next all the more unfortunate. As Rippon reached the pub, the door swung open just as he was about to pull the handle. Standing in front of him were the Garvin brothers and William Furniss. Unaware that he was to be on the receiving end of a beating, but well aware of whom the three men were, Rippon politely stood aside to let the three men past.

What happened next was a lightening assault. Before he could even open his mouth to speak, Rippon was felled by several mighty blows. A razor, a cosh, and a few fists had seen him lose consciousness for a brief moment, but he came round in time to see his three attackers strolling down the road without a care in the world. It was lucky for everybody involved (apart from the attackers) that Rippon had been face to face with them, even only briefly, as he was a man who didn't shy away from the threat of the gangs, and immediately reported the incident to the police. As such, the three men were quickly arrested and taken to the cells of West Bar police station.

It must have been a surprise to them to be joined by the other members of their raiding party. Eyewitnesses had seen some of the other men making their getaway from Princess Street, and as the terrible timeline of events began to fall into place, they were rounded up and arrested for the assault on Jock Plommer.

The policemen on guard struggled to keep order as the gang members kept themselves occupied with rowdy behaviour and raucous singing. However, the mood was about to darken considerably; as the men were about to be informed that they were in much more trouble than they had immediately thought. The desk sergeant asked for some of the men to be brought out of the cells individually, where one by one, they would be informed of Jock

Plommer's death, and their charges changed from assault to murder. There would be no more singing in the cells that night, and all thoughts turned to concocting a believable story.

This was to be a long and difficult night for the prisoners, but nowhere near as difficult as it would be for Mrs Plommer and her four young children. Having been taken to hospital along with her stricken husband, the newly widowed woman would have been formally identifying the body of Jock Plommer as the men had sung and joked in the cells.

The gang warfare had escalated further than it ever had before, and those confined to the West Bar cells were stepping into unchartered territory. They had talked their way out of hundreds of assault charges, but not one of them had ever been involved in anything as serious as the situation in which they now found themselves. Murder, in those days, was punishable by death. There would be no corrupt magistrates or financial punishments this time. The gang had overstepped the mark by a considerable distance, and the only thing that mattered to the eight men in the cells was how they would escape the most serious punishment available to the legal system.

Neither the incarcerated men, nor the Plommer family, would sleep that night, but for very different reasons. The Park Brigade plotted whilst the widow sobbed. This was a night that would change the face of the gang warfare in the city, but one that had also required the ultimate sacrifice to be made. Sooner or later, somebody would have to stand up to the gangs,and that man had been Jock Plommer. Only the Garvin brothers and William Furniss had avoided being charged with murder, as it was assumed that they had been in a different area of the city at the time of the attack on Jock Plommer. However, the story from here on in would take many twists and turns, and nobody would be able to decipher the events of 27 April 1925, for quite some time.

Chapter 9

The Threat of the Black Cap

'Murder is unique in that it abolishes the party it injures, so that society must take the place of the victim, and on his behalf demand atonement or grant forgiveness.'

W.H. Auden, Anglo–American Poet (1907–1973)

It would have appeared to Sam and Bob Garvin that they and Furniss had found themselves on the end of a piece of good fortune. Despite languishing in the cells with their gang mates, the three had not been implicated in the murder of Jock Plommer, as it was incorrectly surmised that they had been in a different area of the city at the time. If anything, their arrest for the attack on Harry Rippon had worked in their favour, as the police had, until now, failed to piece together the timings of the incidents on that particular night, and could only go on the fact that the three had been charged with an assault which took place on the same evening, but in a different district.

In the next two days, the events of 27 April had already been spread around the city by both word of mouth, and also a number of damning articles published in the local press. As the men had yet to stand trial for the attacks, no names had been given at this point, but it was common knowledge amongst the population that this was the work of the Park Brigade. On this occasion, there was to be no ineffective and laughable Magistrates Court trial for the gang members. Their only appearance before a magistrate would to confirm their identities, and be informed that the severity of their crimes could only be dealt with at Leeds Assizes. This also applied to two of the three men who had attacked Harry Rippon, as their luck was about to run out.

Expecting to be bound over or handed a short sentence, the three had taken to the dock on the assault charge, only to be informed that they were to stand trial for murder along with the rest of the gang. It had since been proved that the men could have easily walked from Attercliffe to the Wicker between the attacks, and eyewitnesses had also placed two of them on Princess Street at the time of Jock Plommer's murder. Harry Rippon had actually prepared a statement for the court, in which he testified that Sam Garvin had attacked him with a razor, and Bob Garvin had hit him with some kind of cosh. However, he could not say if William Furniss had played any part. Furniss was also omitted from the eyewitness accounts of the Princess Street residents, and as such, was allowed to leave court a free man. The same could not be said for the Garvin brothers. They had been identified at both attacks, and would now find themselves charged with both assault and murder. They remained in the dock whilst the rest of the gang were brought in, and all seven men were collectively informed that they would be taken to Armley Prison, where they would be held on remand until they could appear before the Leeds Assizes.

The crowd in the public gallery were aghast as the men were held in the dock for a considerable amount of time, before being chained together and led away by a number of police officers, all of whom were armed with revolvers. The gang had gone too far this time, and the chance to levy serious punishment against them had finally presented itself. There was no way that the police were going to let these men out of their sight.

An article which appeared in the *Sheffield Independent* on that same evening shared this mood of outrage and disgust at the murder of Jock Plommer. Credited as being written by 'the Passer By' (possibly due to many gang members still being at large), the article captured the mood of the city:

'Time after time the press has been accused of exaggerating the gang menace in the city, and in cases where some of these hooligans (all of them, by the way, well known to the police) have been accused of savage assaults; the powers that be have invariably shown an amazing leniency.

'True it is, as the City Coroner, Mr Kenyon Parker, observed yesterday, the city has acquired an unenviable notoriety through the prevalence of outrages by one or other of the gangs, and now that public indignation has been thoroughly aroused, there must be no allowing the matter to rest until the canker has been removed, root, and branch, from our midst.

'There is no place for cowardly ruffians in modern civilisation. There is no legal machinery in existence which, if prosecuted with its utmost rigour, would not soon put an end to what has become a veritable reign of terror.

'The Attercliffe crime has brought the government of Sheffield to the bar of public opinion, and , if necessary, those responsible for the city's good name must invoke the aid of the Home Office to secure the assistance necessary to rid it of the excrescence which has flourished for too long.'

As sad and unnecessary as the murder of Jock Plommer had been, it had brought with it some kind of positive legacy, as this had now provided the city with the means to bring the full weight of the law crashing down on the heads of those who had, for so long, been able to flaunt their immoral and violent acts right in front of the eyes of the police. This was in the hands of the Assizes now, and as we have already seen from the sentencing of Sandy Bowler et al, the crown appointed judges of the high courts had no interest in exercising leniency against the gangs, and would allow the Crown Prosecutors to pursue the most severe punishments available.

In this case, the most serious punishment would not involve a long incarceration and hard labour; it would involve the hanging of those who had taken a life, and as nobody had yet to admit to inflicting the fatal stab wounds to Jock Plommer, all of the men chained together in the dock would be held equally responsible in the eyes of the law.

Unravelling the facts of the events which had taken place on 27 April was anything but a simple task. The death itself was an open and closed case, such were the wounds inflicted on Jock Plommer. He had died of the injuries inflicted upon him in the attack which took place in the street outside his house, and this had been confirmed by the necessary post mortem conducted in the case of any violent or suspicious death.

The real difficulty came in finding the truth as to what had occurred on that evening. None of the gang members was interested in implicating one another, and there were no witness statements to confirm which of the men had inflicted the deadly stab wounds. All in all, it took seven days before the case could be satisfactorily unravelled enough for proceedings to be taken to the Assizes.

Each day, the gang members were brought into the Sheffield Police Court under armed guard, having been brought by train from Leeds. A number of constables were also positioned at the court entrance, and in the public gallery, just in case any of the remaining gang members fancied their chances at staging the liberation of the accused men. Despite the witnesses being able to identify the attackers (although not able to ascertain who played what part in the attack), the group of men in the dock staunchly denied their presence at the home of Jock Plommer. Each of the defendants had fabricated their own story, and it was the job of the inquest to pick holes in these false statements.

Wilfred Fowler, Lawrence Fowler, and George Wills freely admitted to being in Attercliffe on that evening, but claimed to have been nowhere near the Plommer house. They had simply taken a stroll, and decided to take a rest outside the fish and chip shop, where they had intended to have some supper before being approached by PC Hogan, who was then called away by a commotion in the distance. Sam Garvin, Bob Garvin, and the absent William Furniss, had been in the Wicker at the time, according to their version of events. The Garvin brothers were more than happy to admit the assault on Harry Rippon (even taking care not to implicate the acquitted Furniss), but still maintained that they had not ventured into Attercliffe on that evening. The remaining men, Frank Kidnew, Fred Goddard, Amos Stewart, Stanley Harker, and William Wild were also happy to admit that they had been up to no good, and had been searching for Arthur Whitham in order to carry out a seperate assault. Yet, like the Garvin brothers, they claimed that they had not been anywhere near Princess Street. This was actually true for a couple of members of the latter group, as the attack on Jock Plommer had been committed by eight men. It would seem that a couple of these men had arrived after the attack on Princess Street, and had found themselves being seen as guilty by association, as they were spotted with the other men later that night.

Also muddying the water was a number of attempts to smear the character of Jock Plommer. These accusations were brought by other members of the Park Brigade who had attended the inquest to provide statements. They were defiant in their oaths that the men in the dock had not murdered Plommer, but were happy to stain his character for extra effect. Accusations against Plommer that were made included a statement that he was a violent and high-ranking member of a nameless rival gang, and had recently committed a number of assaults against various members of the Park Brigade, to which the 'victims' had been of too good a moral character to retaliate. Also mentioned was a story in which it was concocted that Plommer ran a rival tossing Ring, which was situated in a disused garage beneath the Wicker arches. This was quickly refuted by the police, who were happy to confirm that no such place existed, and if it had done, would have been known to them.

Despite the lies and subterfuge, it was decided after a couple of days that the men in the dock were involved in the incident of Princess Street, which, unsurprisingly, led to stories being changed, recollections of the evening suddenly coming back to light, and a swift change in the demeanour of the men in the dock, who had until this point, been in relatively high spirits. It is strange today to hear of reasonable doubt being ascertained or refuted by an inquest, but this was commonplace in the 1920s. An inquest was often used to clear up many of the facts before a case was brought to the high court. However, this practice was abolished by an Act of Parliament just a few years later.

The defendants, most of whom had now suddenly remembered that they *had* been outside the Plommer home on Princess Street, had now begun to turn their minds to mitigation. It was time to let their defence team do the talking on their behalf, as it would be far too easy to contradict themselves by giving separate accounts of the evening. Mr J.W. Fenoughty, the long suffering (but well paid) solicitor for the Park Brigade, took over the reins and chose this time to tell the court of the 'real' events of 27 April in which a bunch of hardened gang members had been so afraid of Jock Plommer that they had travelled to Attercliffe in order to convince him that they did not want any animosity between himself and the gang.

As laughable as this was, the story was about to become far more outrageous, as it was then stated that it was Plommer who had rushed from his house, armed with a razor and a poker, with the sole purpose of attacking the gang, who had knocked politely on his door, and were waiting outside for the chance to offer an olive branch to their tormentor.

All in all, the defence had managed to gather statements from around twenty people, who would all swear that Plommer had been the aggressor. However, most of these statements were made by affiliates of the Park Brigade, and some of them had even been neatly written and signed by men who were barely literate.

One can only imagine that Mr Fenoughty did not hold out much hope for his defence strategy, and after a two-week adjournment for the Whitsuntide holidays, which the gang spent languishing in Armley Prison, it was time for the prosecution to widen the holes which were already appearing in the case for the defence.

It has to be mentioned at this point, that, although this seems like a legal trial, the point of these proceedings was to ascertain who should appear in the high court and on what charges. Nobody could be found guilty or not guilty by the inquest, but the outcome would be of great interest to the judge who would preside over the eventual trial. As such, the prosecution brought in a very important witness, who did not expect to appear at the inquest, but was well prepared to take the stand at the eventual trial. As very little could be done to clear up the events of 27 April, it was the prosecution's intention to leave the inquest with no doubt as to what had occurred on the previous night. Harold Liversidge was brought into the police court by an armed escort. His testimony of the night before the Plommer murder could mean serious repercussions for a couple of the men in the dock, and the police had no intention of allowing this particular witness to be paid off or intimidated. Liversidge could not prove guilt, but he could certainly clear up the question of motive.

The first lie to be uncovered by the prosecution was of minor importance, but spoke volumes to the inquest as to the story concocted by the defence. Liversidge was asked about the claims that Jock Plommer had run an illegal tossing Ring beneath the Wicker arches (and was assisted, one defendant claimed, by Liversidge himself); a claim which he laughingly put to rest.

Revealing to the court that he had been charged with illegal gambling on more than one occasion, both whilst attending the Sky Ring, Liversidge raised the extremely valid point that, if his friend owned a tossing Ring, one which he himself was accused of working at, why would he feel the need to travel to the Sky Ring every time he had fancied an illicit gamble? It was revealed that it was during one of these trips to Park Hill, that Liversidge had become angry about his losses, and had been involved in a brief scuffle with Wilfred Fowler. This, Liversidge reasoned, was probably the reason for the later attack upon him. It was this kind of honest admission which really began to work wonders for the prosecution case. He was then asked to recollect the events on 26 April, and was happy to furnish the inquest with as much information as he could remember. The actual attack had been something of a blur, as he had been taken by surprise, but he clearly remembered hearing the threatening words, 'I am Spinks Fowler, you will remember me,' as he lay in the gutter.

Liversidge then told the story of how he had walked to the home of Jock Plommer, to ask for his assistance. He had originally asked Plommer to join him in a revenge attack, but was turned down by the ex-soldier, who despite his reservations, did promise to accompany him back to the Windsor Hotel, and would ensure that a fair fight was allowed. As for the resulting fight, there was not much to tell, it was simply a fight in the street between two men. Liversidge was physically bigger than Fowler, and had little problem in beating the smaller and younger man into submission. He recalled that

Fowler had received a head wound after falling against the wall during the fight, and at this point, decided that enough was enough.

It was then revealed that the injured Fowler was actually helped to his feet by Plommer, but did not receive any kind of thanks. Instead, he was warned 'Jock, you are in for a tanning for this' and left the scene aided by his older brother. As far as Liversidge and Plommer were concerned; that was an end to the matter, the warning was nothing more than a show of bravado from a defeated man.

These revelations had shifted the spotlight onto the two Fowler brothers, as it provided a strong motive, and also proved that a threat had been made against Plommer. As such, the prosecution spent the remaining days of the inquest concentrating on the interrogation of Wilfred and Lawrence Fowler. These were not only the prime suspects, but also two of the younger and most inexperienced men in the dock. If anyone would crack under pressure, it would surely be them. The older brother, Lawrence, was asked to take the stand to give his version of the incident which had occurred the following day. He claimed that Plommer had produced a poker from his trousers, and had hit Lawrence and his brother over the head with it. He also initially claimed that only he and his brother had been present at the time. The prosecutor, Mr J.E. Wing, quickly leapt upon this statement, and asked for this fact to be confirmed, to which Fowler sheepishly admitted that there had been more men present, but he was not aware of the identity of any of them; something which brought shouts of disbelief from the members of public in the gallery.

Wilfred Fowler took a similar stance, claiming that he and his brother had been assaulted by Plommer, and that neither of them had inflicted a blow of any kind, and also that no other men were present, and if they were, he did not know who they were. This led to the prosecution openly asking Wilfred Fowler how Plommer came to be killed on that night, to which the younger brother responded 'I don't know'.

The chairman of the inquest, Mr Kenyon Parker, had heard enough. The proceedings were becoming a farce, and if none of the defendants were willing to shoulder any of the blame, then they would all stand together in the dock of Leeds Assizes; all under the threat of being found guilty of murder, and with the possibility of being sentenced to death

The funeral of Jock Plommer took place during the period between the inquest and the eventual trial. Such was the public opinion of this honourable and hard-working man, it was estimated that over 8,000 people lined the route from his home in Princess Street to the cemetery at Burngreave. His procession was presided over by the local York and Lancaster Regiment, who were only too proud to carry his coffin, and to march behind the earthly remains of such a legendary soldier. To the sound of bagpipes Plommer was taken to his final resting place and the city as a whole had taken time to reflect upon his cruel and needless death. A fund was organised for the grieving Plommer family by the Bessemer Company and the local regiment, which reportedly raised a great deal of money for the family. The city had stood by their side, and the tragic death of their husband and father was mourned by thousands. No longer would the people of Sheffield allow the mindless acts of violence to go unpunished.

Shamefully, there had been a few incidents during the funeral parade. Members of the Park Brigade had attended, and did their best to disrupt things. However, a few plain clothes policemen and a few thousand outraged mourners soon put paid to the distasteful antics, and their cries of innocence for their colleagues were swiftly silenced.

A statement in the *Sheffield Mail* appeared in that night's edition, and captured the mood of the city in a brief, yet succinct manner:

> 'On many sides one heard remarks of indignation at the cruel death which had befallen Mr Plommer, and the huge crowds which gathered in all parts strikingly demonstrates the intense sympathy which the citizens of Sheffield have accorded to the relatives of the dead man.'

The sense of outrage was so great that it was no surprise to find that plans of vigilante justice were being discussed. A number of ex-servicemen had reportedly vowed to crush the Park Brigade, and any other gang which threatened the safety of the city streets, yet, in a public statement, the Chief Constable, John Hall Dalwood pleaded for calm and urged the public to let the judicial system deal with the gangs. This was to be one of the last official acts of the man who had struggled so greatly to free the city of the seemingly untouchable gangs of thugs. He would soon be replaced by a less media savvy, yet more decisive replacement. The tide had begun to turn, and one can only imagine that Hall-Dalwood was only too pleased to be relieved of his thankless duty.

Despite public feeling, the Park Brigade had not yet been vanquished. The following two weeks between the inquest and the trial saw a number of attacks, which were committed by the remaining members. Some of these were revenge attacks, but others were deliberate attempts to intimidate witnesses. Arthur Whitham, who had narrowly escaped being attacked along with Plommer and Rippon on the night of 27 April had been chatting with a policeman in Attercliffe one evening, only to be felled by a mighty punch from Park Brigade member Ernest Broomhead, who had taken his chance to strike when his prey was otherwise engaged.

Broomhead was drunk at the time, which would explain assaulting someone as they chatted to a policeman, and was easily tackled by the constable, who was able to call for assistance and ensure that Broomhead appeared before the magistrates the next morning where he was fined £5 after insisting that the assault was due to a 'personal matter', rather than being on behalf of the gang. Whitham himself was not actually to appear at the trial, but unaware of this, the Park brigade still continued to target him. A young member of the gang, Arthur Jackson had threatened to 'do him in' during an altercation in the street, but without the necessary backup, the young man was forced to retreat sheepishly as the physically impressive Whitham rounded upon him and invited him to try his luck. The intimidation had also occurred during the inquest, with a number of witnesses being followed onto a tram by gang members, who found themselves being thrown off the tram by plain clothes police officers who had been tasked with ensuring the safety of the witnesses. Whether the tram was in motion at the time was sadly never recorded.

As the trial approached, the city began to reach fever pitch, especially as it had been reported by the local newspapers that Mr J.W Fenoughty had confirmed that all ten of his clients would be pleading not guilty. The upcoming trial was the talk of the town, and only quick and decisive justice would be enough to quash the sense of injustice which had been prevalent in the city for so long, but had now reached breaking point.

Chapter 10

Truth, Half-Truths, and Lies

'I believe that truth has only one face: that of a violent contradiction.'

Georges Bataille, French Novelist and Philosopher (1897–1962)

The trial which began on 28 July was unusual, as there were so many defendants and the guilty party or parties had not been identified as delivering the fatal wounds to Jock Plommer. As such, all ten men stood accused of 'being concerned in the wilful murder of William Francis Plommer'. The ten men in the dock were: Samuel Garvin, 45, Heavygate Avenue; Robert Garvin, 36, Allen Street; Frank Kidnew, 40, Campo Lane; Lawrence Fowler, 25, Ardmore Street; Wilfred Fowler, 23, Stevenson Road; George Wills, 22, Cyclops Street; Fred Goddard, 18, Stevenson Road; Amos Stewart, 21, March Street; Stanley Harker, 23, Leigh Street; William Wild, 28, Brightside Lane.

As had been the approach in Sheffield, the security arrangements at Leeds Town Hall, where the Assizes were taking place, were strict and highly organised. All entrances and exits were guarded by police constables, and many more plain clothes officers were posted around the building to ensure that there was no interference with the trial or the witnesses. Additional carriages were added to the 8am train from Sheffield to Leeds, where eighty witnesses would be protected by police on both legs of the journey. Another carriage was also reserved for members of the press and police officials. These arrangements were to be repeated for each day of the trial. The prisoners themselves were also under close protection, as the threats made by the ex-servicemen of Sheffield had been taken extremely seriously. Their route to court was changed each day, and they were accompanied on every journey by a number of armed policemen. Their safety was guaranteed, but any escape was impossible.

Mr Mortimer, prosecuting, opened the proceedings by describing the injuries inflicted upon the deceased. He read from the hospital report which listed 'three head wounds, all of which were around an inch in length, and were so violent that they had reached the skull' which were serious injuries, but had not been the cause of death. That had been 'internal haemorrhaging caused by two stab wounds to the stomach, both deliberately inflicted'. It was surmised that either of the wounds would have been enough to kill Plommer, and that he had stood no chance at all of recovering from his injuries, even if he had been admitted to hospital within seconds of the attack. It was also detailed in the report that a large number of other superficial wounds were present, all of which bore the signs of being delivered by a different weapon and a different hand. A short bayonet was the probable murder weapon, yet Jock Plommer had found himself subjected to a vicious and deliberate attack in which he was wounded by several men, and several weapons.

The two nights' events were then shared in great detail for the benefit of the court. These included the assault on Liversidge, the subsequent beating of Wilfred Fowler, and the threats made by the defeated man towards Plommer. These facts were already well known to the majority of the courtroom, but some of the details from 27 April were not. It came to light that earlier in the afternoon that Lawrence Fowler had been spotted by many witnesses wandering round Attercliffe. During this time, he went into a number of shops and pubs to ask where Plommer lived. Having seemingly found his answer, Fowler was seen leaving the area, only to return later with several more men.

It was also reported that Sam Garvin had approached a man in Attercliffe at around 7:45pm, and had asked if he knew where Spud Murphy lived. Although not directly connected to the incident of the previous night, Murphy had been present when Wilfred Fowler was felled by Liversidge, and the Mooney Gang member was said to have mocked the brothers as they left the area. This was a fact not divulged during the inquest, but would explain why Garvin was so full of bloodlust on that night. He would normally have stayed out of the way, but on this occasion, decided to join his men on the front line. The man Garvin had approached, Mr Day, was invited to the stand, where he would reveal that Garvin said, 'There has been some trouble, and them what has done it will pay for it. We'll cut him [Murphy] into pieces, and Jock as well.' This was just a few minutes before the gang arrived at Plommer's house, and is also where the story begins to unravel. A witness, a miner named Holmes, reported seeing the Garvin brothers, along with Kidnew and Wild, board a tram. Mr Holmes then saw the remaining six men walk back to the Plommer house, where they began to call for the occupant to come out and face them.

The court was told that Plommer had left his house and walked across to the group of men almost immediately. It was also confirmed that he was carrying no weapon of any kind, contrary to some of the statements which had been made by the gang. He simply strode across the street with his thumbs in his waistcoat pockets, perfectly happy to stand his ground.

Holmes then told the court that he had called out to Plommer, shouting something along the lines of 'For God's sake, Jock, clear out!' to which Plommer replied, 'I'll just have to stick it.' The six men then descended upon Plommer, who held out his arms and calmly said, 'If it's a fair fight, I'll take you one by one.' His request was ignored, and it was Lawrence Fowler who spoke for the gang, spitting, 'You've done our kid, and we're going to do you,' before raising his fists to attack Plommer, who wasted absolutely no time in knocking the older Fowler brother to the ground with one punch. This was the spark which lit the tinderbox and within seconds all six men were attacking Plommer.

Holmes recalled that Lawrence Fowler had got back up as the rest of the gang set about Plommer, and took this opportunity to deliver a blow to the back of his head with a poker while he was otherwise engaged. Still the mighty oak would not fall and it was not until several more blows had been inflicted with pokers and a cosh that the former soldier eventually collapsed to the ground.

This version of events was backed up by several more witness statements, as many of Plommer's neighbours had observed the terrible scenes from the safety of their own houses. Sadly, one such witness was Plommer's 12-year-old son, who was able to tell the police that one of the men had hit his dad with a 'truncheon'.

Every witness was able positively to identify the men they saw as the men in the dock, with the exceptions of the Garvin brothers, Frank Kidnew and William Wild. It was becoming clear that some of the defendants were in a lot more trouble than the others.

One detail in the testimony of Mr Holmes had caused a stir in the courtroom. He mentioned that he had seen Lawrence Fowler making a jabbing motion towards Plommer's stomach as he lay face up on the ground. This was also confirmed by two other witnesses, one of whom said that it was at this point that Plommer's mouth fell open, and his arms, which had been raised to protect himself from the blows, fell by his sides. It was at this moment that a car turned into Princess Street and stopped to see what was happening in the road. The passenger, who did not want to appear in court, but had been happy to provide a written statement, was adamant that he had seen Wilfred Fowler brandishing a weapon, which he described as 'a short flat blade, like a small bayonet'. The man in the car then went on to describe how Plommer had managed to struggle to his feet, and tried to climb onto the car, but fell, and then managed to crawl back to the doorway of his house. It was during these final few seconds that Wilfred Fowler picked up the child's scooter, and crashed it into Plommer's head, before the gang turned on their heels and made their getaway.

These witness statements, which had, until now, been kept secret so that witnesses could testify without fear of reprisal, had been instrumental in piecing together the timeline of the attack. They also cast very serious light as to the involvement of the Fowler brothers. Several people had seen Lawrence Fowler seemingly stabbing Plommer, and had also seen Wilfred Fowler in possession of a short bayonet (of the kind used by some German soldiers during the recent war). As such, the Fowler brothers were in even more trouble, having already been earmarked as the main aggressors during the recent inquest. Things were bound to get worse for them by the end of the trial, as this had only been the first day of the proceedings, and there were still many more witnesses to follow.

PC Hogan was then called to the stand. He recalled his brief conversation with the Fowler brothers and George Wills, which was interrupted by the cries of Mrs Plommer. For the first time, details of this exchange were made public, and, again, the Fowler brothers found the long arm of the law wrapping itself further around their throats. The reason for going over to the three men, Hogan recalled, was that he thought he saw George Wills quickly slip a razor into his pocket as the policeman walked by. He also told the court that he thought that at least one of the brothers had a considerable amount of blood on his hands, but told the policeman that he had just cut himself. This, in a way, was true. Wilfred Fowler did have a deep cut to his finger, which had probably been caused by mishandling either the bayonet or a razor. However, no further explanation was to be required, as it was at this point that Mrs Plommer's cries echoed through the street, and Hogan turned on his heels and ran to investigate the commotion.

It was at this point that Mr Mortimer, prosecuting, took the opportunity to remind the jury that there were currently ten men in the dock, and although it seemed that the Fowler brothers were the main culprits, the other eight men still had serious charges to answer. The brothers would now be tried for murder, but the charges against the other men would still stand:

'The case for the prosecution is that the fatal blow was by the hands of Wilfred and Lawrence Fowler, or, certainly by one of them.

As regards the others, the case for the prosecution is that they had joined the party; that they had a common purpose; and although the weapons they used did not lead to Plommer's death, the other four, having assisted in the attack and having played their own part in it alongside others, are equally guilty of murder, in the eyes of the law, as Lawrence and Wilfred Fowler.'

With this, the court adjourned until the next day. If the prosecution were to have their way, they would send all ten men to the gallows. The jury were allowed to leave under guard, and the witnesses were escorted to their specially arranged train. As for the ten defendants, they were chained together and bundled into a police van which would deliver them back to their cells in Armley Prison.

The next morning, the prosecution had chosen to bring one of their most important witnesses to the stand. Mrs Plommer had been called as the first witness of the day so that she could leave the court after her testimony should she wish to. A respectful hush descended over the public gallery as she took the oath, and steeled herself to give her version of the nightmarish events of 27 April. She confirmed that her husband had left the house between 7:45 and 7:50 that evening, and that his reason for doing so was to see what the commotion in the street was about. She also swore on oath that her husband was empty handed when leaving the house, and had no weapons of any kind about his person.

Worried about her husband, Mrs Plommer had stood on the doorway as he approached the men, and described how 'the one with the bandages' (Wilfred Fowler) had been the main aggressor, while the other men gathered around her husband. It was then that Lawrence Fowler took the lead in the argument, only to be floored by a single punch from her husband. It was at this point that the whole scene descended into chaos, with many blows being delivered by many hands. She had started to make her way towards the melee as her husband fell to the ground, but stopped as she noticed the pokers and razors in the hands of the attackers. She then saw the blood running down her husband's side, and heard Lawrence Fowler shouting 'Come on, let's finish him!' The car then arrived in the street, and the men started to back away, allowing her husband to struggle to his feet, only to fall to his knees and attempt to crawl back to the house. Wilfred Fowler then smashed the metal scooter into the back of his head, before all of the men started to run away.

As Mrs Plommer's statement had been a carbon copy of the statement which was read out at the inquest there was very little in the way of cross-examination. Mr Streatfield, defending the two Fowler brothers, had tried to push her into admitting that her husband had helped to attack Wilfred Fowler on 26 April, but she reaffirmed the circumstances as had been explained to her by her husband, and which had also been backed up by Harold Liversidge and Spud Murphy.

Mrs Plommer was then replaced in the witness box by Frank Griffiths, a shopkeeper from Princess Street, who had been able to observe the incident from his premises. Griffiths echoed much of what Mrs Plommer had told the court, but added that four of the men reached into their pockets for weapons as Jock had fallen to the ground. He went on to say that he was certain that Jock Plommer had been unarmed, and each of the other men was carrying at least one weapon. 'It was a dastardly and cowardly attack' he said 'committed by a bunch of absolute f....' before being told to silence himself immediately by the judge, Mr Justice Findlay.

Another important witness for the prosecution was William Hazlewood, who had been in the area after meeting a friend for a drink on his way home from work. He reported seeing Plommer walking towards the group of men, and again, confirmed that Plommer was unarmed. His recollection of the attack was very similar to those that had testified before him, but he was able to add that he saw one of the men making 'a stabbing motion'. Hazlewood claimed that it was a man in a light suit that had made this lunge, and confirmed that to the best of his recollection, the man in the light suit was Lawrence Fowler. It was certainly true that the older Fowler brother had been wearing a light suit when arrested, and that the other men were wearing darker clothing.

All in all, the witnesses had agreed on most of the major points, with very few variations. However, it was to be Mrs Rose Lemm, who had also appeared at the inquest, who would create the biggest gasp from the public gallery, as she swore on oath that she had seen Lawrence Fowler stab Plommer while the two wrestled on the floor, and that she had subsequently seen Wilfred Fowler putting a bladed weapon into a long black case before the men had made their getaway.

The last witness was to be Dr J.E. Schofield, who had attended Plommer at the Royal Infirmary. It had been Dr Schofield's report which had been read out at the inquest, and he did not deviate from his written statement in any way during his time in the witness box. His delivery of the facts was professional and completely without emotion:

'There were two large wounds to the abdomen, and the clothing had been cut through. Parts of the internal organs were also protruding. There were also three scalp wounds which were clean down to the bone, caused by a razor or poker.

The severe abdominal wounds could not have been caused by a razor, but a weapon similar to, or smaller than, a bayonet. The cause of death was internal haemorrhaging and shock.'

Cross-examined by Mr Mortimer for the defence, Dr Schofield was asked why there were very few other marks on the body of Jock Plommer, despite the savagery of the attack as described by the witnesses. Dr Schofield replied that, due to the amount of blood loss, bruising would be diminished, and that bruises would not appear after death.

The next morning, the ten defendants arrived at court in ten different taxi cabs, all of them being accompanied by their own armed guard. This was to be the day when the tables would be turned, and the defence counsel would be given their chance to give their own version of events, and to challenge the damning evidence which had been laid out before the court. Mr J.W. Jardine, defending the four men who denied being present during the attack on Plommer, took the opportunity to make his case early in the morning. Not one witness had put them at the scene of the crime, and three of the men would freely admit that they were 'otherwise occupied' with Harry Rippon at the time.

This was contested by the prosecution, who reminded the judge that an earlier witness had told the court that Sam Garvin had claimed to have 'got a mob' to join him in attacking Jock Plommer. Whether he had been there or not, as leader of the gang, the older Garvin brother had still played a major part in the crime. As such, Frank Kidnew and William Wild were acquitted, and allowed to return to the prison where their immediate release would be organised. Harry Rippon had failed to implicate Kidnew in his assault, as he could not remember him striking a blow against him, so there were no charges remaining against him, and William Wild seems to have been especially unlucky, as it would seem that he went home after initially joining with the posse, and had spent three months in Armley Prison due to being 'guilty by association.'

Bob Garvin was removed from the dock for these proceedings, but was returned to his prison cell to await the trial for his alleged assault on Harry Rippon. Sam Garvin was denied any such leniency, and was told by the judge that he would stand trial alongside the men 'who had been under his control' at the time of the murder. The gang leader was the first of the men to be called to the witness box, and when asked to recount the events of that night, simply stated that he was not there. He also denied knowing some of the men who appeared in the dock alongside him. His testimony had been a waste of everybody's time, as not one word of truth had been given.

Mr Mortimer, cross-examining asked Garvin if he had 'laid the trail, and then endeavoured to save your own skin by getting away from the place,' to which Garvin replied, 'I've told you already, I know nothing about it.' With a sense of exasperation, Mr Mortimer allowed Garvin to return to the dock. The next of the defendants to step into the witness box was Lawrence Fowler, who claimed to have been at the races in Uttoxeter on the day in question and only found out about the fight in which his brother had been injured upon returning home that evening. Fowler's recollection of the incident was largely a direct contrast to that of the endless stream of eyewitnesses. He claimed that he and his brother had been strolling through Attercliffe, when they had been accosted by Plommer, who was brandishing a poker and a razor. He admitted that a fight did take place, but that he had no idea how Plommer came to receive the stab wounds.

To make his story even less convincing, Fowler mentioned the other men at the fight, but had previously stated that only himself, his brother, and Plommer had been present. He also went on to deny that he knew any of the other men, and that none of the other men in the dock had been present on that evening, apart from his brother. Having successfully cross-examined himself, there was little need for Mr Mortimer to spend any more time exposing the falsehoods of Fowler's statement, and he was allowed to return to the dock, where he would swap places with his younger brother. Wilfred Fowler was the next to take the stand.

The younger Fowler brother began by describing the events of 26 April. He claimed that he had been involved in 'a fair fight' with Harold Liversidge, whom he had supposedly defeated, but then was attacked by Plommer, who had brought a poker with him. He also claimed that, the next day, he had been made aware that Plommer had offered £20 to Fowler if he could defeat him in a fight; that was why he and his brother had been in Attercliffe. His version of events was a carbon copy of his brother's, insisting that Plommer had been armed, and was the main aggressor on this occasion. He also claimed that he had no idea how Plommer came to be stabbed, adding that it must have happened after the fight, and that the culprit must have taken the opportunity to 'stab Jock, and lay the blame on the Park boys.'

One by one, the defendants told their unlikely tales, agreeing in the most part, but often slipping up and deviating from the rehearsed script. All in all, the case for the defence had been flimsy at best, and with almost eighty witnesses to dispute their stories, it looked like the Park Brigade were finally about to get their comeuppance.

The fourth and final day of the trial began with a curious show of subterfuge, as several taxis, a few horse-drawn carriages, and a large van arrived at the town hall. What made this more unusual is that none of the vehicles had contained any of the defendants, who had been placed into five private cars and quickly whisked through one of the rear entrances to the building.

The first business to attend to was the testimony of 18-year-old Fred Goddard, who lived with Wilfred Fowler, and had only been identified as being present during the attack by one of the many witnesses. Goddard's solicitor, Dr E.C. Chappell, read out a statement in which he pleaded with the court to exonerate his client, and spare him from the rest of the proceedings.

> 'This unfortunate boy finds himself here on what must be to him one of the most terrible crimes. By this time, I am sure that you will have formed the conclusion that if Wilfred Fowler had not taken him in as a lodger, he would not now be in this position.'

Replying for the prosecution, Mr Mortimer stated that if Goddard was not guilty, then the jury would find him so. This was also the opinion of the judge, who ruled that Goddard should stay in the dock, and would be allowed to leave immediately if no guilty verdicts were brought against him. The judge was not prepared to take any chances in such a serious case.

With all of the witness statements and testimonies out of the way, all that was left was for the two opposing counsels to complete their summing up. As is still the case in the English legal system, the prosecution were called upon to state their case first. Mr Mortimer laid out a simple equation. There had been almost eighty eyewitness testimonies which had corroborated the case for the prosecution, whereas, the only evidence for the defence was the testimonies of the defendants themselves, who had frequently contradicted each other and their solicitors. Also outstanding was a simple question, 'If none of the men her present was responsible for stabbing Mr Plommer, how did he come to die of stab wounds on the night of 27 April 27?' Had any of the men taken responsibility, he added, then there would not have been as many people in the dock at the present time.

The summing up for the defence would be a more complicated matter, as the seven men remaining in the dock were represented by four different defence counsels. For the sake of brevity, Dr Chappell chose not to perform a lengthy summing up for his client, Fred Goddard, and simply reiterated that his client should not be found guilty of any charges.

Not so brief was the summing up of Mr Streatfield, representing the Fowler brothers. His only real line of defence was that several of the many witnesses had not claimed to have seen either of his clients in possession of a bladed weapon. The brothers, he admitted, were willing to plead guilty to manslaughter, but he claimed that there was still sufficient doubt against his clients, so a guilty verdict should not be reached without a maximum amount of consideration.

Mr A. Burnand had not featured a great deal in the proceedings, as he was defending Wills, Stewart and Harker, who had been seen as little more than bit part players in the whole affair. He appealed to the jury that any gathering of a few men in Sheffield was considered gang related in the current climate, and urged the jury to 'shut all ideas of gangs out of your minds altogether.' If his clients *had* been involved in the fracas, then they had done nothing more than brawl in the street, and, while this was a crime in itself, was not serious enough for them to have been subjected to murder charges. If the jury found them guilty, then 'they could be convicted of nothing more than manslaughter in this unfortunate incident'.

Last to speak was Mr J.W. Jardine. He had already seen three of his clients being allowed to leave the dock, but was still there to represent Sam Garvin. His case relied on the fact that Garvin was not present during the incident, and that no evidence had been brought which proved his client to have ordered the attack upon the deceased. Although he had made threats, Garvin could not be found guilty as an accessory if he had not even been present at the time. The assault on Harry Rippon was another case altogether, and his client was happy to stand trial for something he had admittedly done, but only found himself in the dock at the present time due to conjecture and hearsay.

The summing up, although only briefly described in these pages, had actually taken up most of the day. However, to save everybody from making another trip to the court on the following day, the judge decided that he would extend the proceedings a little longer in order for the trial to come to an end.

Having allowed the proceedings to be extended, one would have expected Mr Justice Findlay to be brief with his own summing up, yet it took three and a half hours for the experienced judge to go over all of the evidence and offer his thoughts on the case that had been brought before him. Finally reaching the business end of his speech, the judge reminded the jury that six of the seven men had been implicated in the fight by many witnesses, and as such, each of them had played a part in the incident which led to the death of Jock Plommer. As for Sam Garvin, it was likely that he was not present at the time, but it was for the jury to decide whether the gang had acted upon his orders, and that he possessed sufficient power over the group for them to have acted on his behalf, adding that 'mere malevolence is not sufficient to convict any man.' In the case of the Fowler brothers, Mr Justice Findlay reminded the court that there had been no irrefutable evidence to convict the two of murder, but a large amount of eyewitness testimony had placed them at the scene, and had suggested that both of them were seen handling a bladed weapon during the fracas.

As reaction to his impassioned speech began to die down, the judge took the opportunity to advise the jury to consider each defendant separately, and to try to look upon the proceedings as several separate cases. Only this, he added, could ensure that the greatest amount of thought was given to the situation of each man. While the judge had droned on for over three hours, the jury wasted very little time in their deliberations. The future of seven men was decided in just under 45 minutes, which equates to just six minutes per man; more than enough time to weigh up the charges against the peripheral defendants, but worryingly brief for those who could still find themselves at the end of a rope.

There was a great sense of excitement in the courtroom as it was announced that the jury was returning. A fight for seats ensued, and a large number of reporters seemed to appear from nowhere brandishing notepads and pencils. This was the moment that an entire city had been waiting for. The chairman of the jury confirmed that decisions had been reached in all cases, and that agreement had been unanimous regarding every charge. The public gallery fell silent as the verdicts were delivered, and each man in the dock took his turn in standing to receive his punishment.

Garvin and Goddard were found not guilty of murder or manslaughter, and Goddard was tearful as he was allowed to leave the dock. Garvin, however, still had the lesser charge of the assault on Harry Rippon hanging over him, and as such, was returned to Armley to join his brother and await a new trial date. Wills, Stewart and Harker were found guilty of manslaughter, and were all to receive lengthy custodial sentences. Harker, with no previous convictions, was sentenced to seven years imprisonment, while the more hardened gang men, Wills and Stewart, were each sentenced to ten years penal servitude. This was a harsh sentence, but was far more agreeable than the punishment which could have been handed down to them.

With their friends having been removed from the dock, the Fowler brothers now stood alone. Witness testimony and circumstantial evidence had created a compelling case against them, and only the leniency of the judge could save them from this point onwards.

Lawrence Fowler was the first to be addressed. 'How say you, do you find Lawrence Fowler guilty of murder or not guilty?'

'Guilty'

The older brother slumped into his chair as his younger sibling was then instructed to stand.

'Do you find Wilfred Fowler guilty of murder or not guilty?

'Guilty'

Within seconds, the two men were surrounded by warders, who instructed them both to stand at the rails in order to receive their sentences. The outcome was almost inevitable, but there was still a great collective gasp from the public gallery as the black cap was placed on upon the wig of Mr Justice Findlay.

A life had been cruelly taken, and the punishment for such a crime was to be hanged by the neck until dead. The brothers stared impassively as the death sentence was passed upon them both, and for a few seconds, the court was left in a state of shocked silence. The silence was broken by Lawrence Fowler, who screamed from the dock 'I spoke the truth, I am innocent. If his wife would only speak the truth ... It is an impossible decision.'

With that, the two brothers were led away from the dock, only to be transported to the condemned cells of Armley Prison. The city of Sheffield had demanded real justice, and it would appear that, on this occasion, the law had found a way to combat the Sheffield gangs.

Chapter 11

Fighting Fire with Fire

'Oh judge! Your damn laws! The good people don't need them,
and the bad people don't obey them.'

Ammon Hennasy, Irish-American Social Activist (1893–1970)

A t this point of the story, it becomes necessary to go back in time by
a few weeks. We have studied in detail the events which took place
in Leeds, but in many ways, the goings-on in Sheffield whilst the
defendants were languishing in Armley Prison were just as important, and
would prove to be an integral part of the wider story. The funeral of Jock
Plommer had brought the city folk out in their thousands to say goodbye to
somebody who had stood up to the gangs. Most had never met him, but he
represented all that was good in the city, and had been taken from his family
by the very men who were feared by each and every man, woman, and child
who had lined the funeral route.

Despite his warning to the public that vigilante justice would not be
tolerated, faith was beginning to be lost in Chief Constable Hall-Dalwood,
who was regarded by many as being nothing more than a public relations
specialist. He could write a good speech, but had delivered very few of his
promises, and was far too insipid for many of the local politicians and leading
businessmen. The city was crying out for an effective leader, but very few
were content to put their trust in Hall-Dalwood or the local council. The
slums were still in existence, unemployment was still rife, and the threat of
the gangs was still a major factor in Sheffield life, despite several leading
members of the Park Brigade being held in Armley Prison.

The local press had been instrumental in stirring up a mood of discontent,
even the newspapers which had previously been sympathetic towards
the Chief Constable and his plight. The time had come for the people of
Sheffield to take back the city, and anyone in high office who tried to play
down the sense of unrest was politely asked by the journalists to reconsider
their position.

For most people, the main concern was that the gangs had now proven that they were willing to kill, and the arrest and imprisonment of Garvin and his men did little to subdue the fear amongst the working class. Ten men had been removed from the streets for the time being, but for each man languishing in Armley, there were another ten to take his place. If anything, the Park Brigade was becoming more unruly without its leading figures. The number of serious and organised crimes would drop slightly, but a rise would be seen in the number of street robberies and petty thefts. This was due to the work of the junior gang members, who now found themselves without a natural leader, but still able to rely on their many gang mates for assistance.

The one positive aspect of the emergence of the reformed Mooney Gang, albeit without its eponymous leader, was that for the last few months, the gangs had only targeted each other. But, with nobody to organise these planned attacks, the city became a bit of a free for all in the eyes of the younger thugs. In reality, the police were simply faced with ten less gang members to keep an eye on. They were still run ragged by bouts of petty crime and common assaults, and were also charged with being on the lookout for any suspected vigilante groups. They were as understaffed and hard-working as ever, and something had to change before the city descended into chaos once again.

With the gangs officially leaderless, the time was right to strike while the iron was hot. However, due to the reluctance of Hall-Dalwood to take any decisive action, and the magistrates still performing their duties with the minimum of effort, it seemed as if the chance effectively to combat the gangs was about to be lost. In the end, it was an order that came from far above the head of Hall-Dalwood that would bring change in the way the gangs were handled. No longer would they be 'kept an eye on' or 'left to the mercy of the magistrates'; it was time to fight fire with fire. The city called for a firm hand, and before long, it would have more than one strong grasp available to keep the citizens of Sheffield safe.

Hall-Dalwood had received a telegram from the Home Secretary, William Joynson-Hicks, in which he had been instructed to form a squad which would be capable of suppressing the gangs. This was to be a small unit with the run of the whole city, and should only include those who were ready and willing to tackle the gang violence with an iron fist.

Joynson-Hicks, who was also the 1st Viscount Brentford, was known as a strict authoritarian. He had been a solicitor in his professional career, before becoming a member of parliament for Manchester North West. On his rise to the top, he had notably defeated Winston Churchill in a local by-election, and was seen by his Prime Minister, Stanley Baldwin, as being perfect for the role of Home Secretary. Despite his reputation as 'Baldwin's Bulldog', Joynson-Hicks was a man willing to accept change and progress. He was a firm believer in law and order, and was notoriously critical of the nightclub and 'flapper' generation, yet he was a man who, more often than not, had the interest of the nation at heart. He was responsible for piloting the Representation of the People Act, 1928, which gave women exactly the same voting rights as men, and was also at the epicentre of many changes made in the legal system, such as reforming the Borstal system, and ruling that every court in the land should have a resident probation officer.

During his tenure, Joynson-Hicks also visited every prison in the British Isles, making notes and asking to see every inch of these institutions. It was under his leadership that the conditions in many prisons went from being Victorian hell-holes, to more modern and forward-thinking establishments. He was perfectly willing to take the strongest action possible against the enemies of the nation, but was also keen to offer a chance of reformation to even the most hardened criminals. As a veteran of the First World War, serving as a high-ranking officer with the Middlesex Regiment, Joynson-Hicks was also a man trusted by the people. He kept abreast of news from all parts of the nation, which is exactly how he came to involve himself in tackling the gang culture which had become prevalent in Sheffield.

His order to Hall-Dalwood had been given for the good of the city, and was exactly the kind of assistance which the Chief Constable had asked for in previous years. Yet, with it being public knowledge that the order was given over his head, it has often been reported that Hall-Dalwood saw this as the beginning of the end of his career with the police.

On 1 May 1925, a new police unit was unleashed on the city. Their chief, and sole, aim was to act as a constant barrier between the gangs and the public, and they were afforded the opportunity to use any means possible to tackle the gangs and their crimes. The four men selected for the unit had been hand-picked by the higher echelons of the police, and had been chosen due to their dedication to the job, their physical size, and their determination to carry out their duties by whatever means were necessary. The police were about to unleash their own hired muscle onto the city streets.

The man who had been chosen to lead the four-man unit was Detective Sergeant William Robinson. He had been a serving police officer for 15 years, and before that, was an officer in the Coldstream Guards. He was less physically imposing than the men in his charge, but came with a fierce reputation, and would have no hesitation in risking his own life in the line of duty. PC Walter Loxley was the biggest physical threat on the team. He was 6ft 3in tall, and weighed almost 20 stone. He had also been brought in from the Central City Division, which mean that he was no stranger to dealing with violent crime. Loxley was a war veteran, and had earned the title of Champion Shell Carrier with the Royal Garrison Artillery. It is reported that Loxley's party trick was to hold seven tennis balls in one of his huge hands. Smaller than Loxley, but with more than enough might to tackle even the hardest gang member, was PC Herbert Lunn. An ex-heavyweight boxer, Lunn had joined the police in 1912, and had served as one of the most renowned 'crushers' in the police force for thirteen years, save for his service in the war, in which he had been awarded a medal for rescuing wounded soldiers under fire. The last member was PC Jack Farrily, the youngest member of the team, but a physically impressive young man who had been raised in the slums of Sheffield, and was no stranger to an alehouse fight or a back alley brawl. This was a man who would think nothing of wading into the most dangerous situation, which had earned him the nickname of 'Fearless Jack'.

All four men could now say goodbye to their uniforms, as their job now involved spending their days in pubs and gambling dens. They were tasked with bringing as much trouble to the gangs as possible, and would remove the gang members from any establishment they happened to wander into. The gang men would no longer be allowed to feel comfortable in any part of the city. An important part of the task was to make themselves known to every innkeeper and landlord in the city. They would offer their own protection against the gangs, but would not tolerate any harbouring of undesirable characters in the pubs and clubs. The idea behind this was to stop the gangs from meeting up, therefore quashing any plans which could be made in the comfort of a taproom or snug.

It was a matter of days before the reputation of the 'Special Duties Squad' had swept across the city. Amongst the law-abiding city folk, the four men were seen as almost minor celebrities. Men, woman and children would shout to them as they passed, hoping for a wave in return. However, they were no so welcomed by the gangs.

Their instructions to suppress the gangs by any means possible had been met with some opposition from various defence solicitors, who feared that these new job roles gave the squad a license to use violence without fear of consequences. This was indeed true, but as the orders had come from the

Home Secretary himself, there was very little that could be done about it. The squad was permitted to use 'all necessary force', yet, only they in their job roles could realistically define what was necessary and what wasn't in each situation. The police did not want deaths on their hands, but were more than happy to overlook a few broken noses and black eyes inflicted during their duties. The four were also permitted to carry weapons, as it was common knowledge that they would find themselves up against pokers and razors on a daily basis. They carried truncheons, as did the rest of the police, but their weapons were shorter and heavier than those carried by the regular constables. This enabled the squad to keep their weapons hidden until it was time to use them.

Although officially titled the Special Duties Squad, the men were also known on the streets as the Flying Squad, such was their talent for arriving at the scene of a gang crime seemingly at the drop of a hat. This was a phrase first coined in 1919 by the Metropolitan police, who had created the first rapid response team in order to keep up with the local miscreants. However, it wasn't luck or speed which aided the swift arrivals, it was intelligence.

The four men had spent much of their time amongst the gang members, and prided themselves on identifying a weak link. The less effective gang men would then be approached at a later date, and told in no uncertain terms that they were now to become informants of the Flying Squad. Very few resisted, and those who did found themselves bruised, bandaged, and before the magistrates. This led to a number of complaints made against the squad, most of which were summarily dismissed. However, there were occasions where allegations had been made against the four men, and it was the duty of the magistrates to decide whether then men in the dock had been criminals or victims.

One of the first gang members to report his rough treatment was the hardened gangster, George Ganner Wheywell, who was now one of the leading members of the reformed Mooney Gang. He had found himself in court for an assault on PC Lunn, but was adamant that it was the policemen who should have been in the dock.

On 21 September, Wheywell had been drinking in a local pub, the Red House, when three members of the Flying Squad had entered. They pointed out several men to the landlord, and advised him that they should be asked to leave, or they would do his job for him. One of these men was Wheywell, who took exception to being thrown out of a pub for no reason.

It was explained to Wheywell by PC Lunn that they would not permit any gang members to assemble in public places, and that if he did not leave the premises of his own accord; he would do so 'head first'. This was a red rag to a bull, and Ganner Wheywell threw what was perhaps the most foolish punch of his life. The punch landed on the eye socket of PC Lunn, who barely flinched. Within seconds, Wheywell was on the ground having been knocked senseless by Lunn; he was then dragged to his feet and propelled through the door and headlong onto the pavement by Loxley and Farrily. With this, the other gang members stood up and left the pub without a word.

Having been arrested and appearing in court for throwing the punch at PC Lunn, Wheywell was a sorry sight in the dock. He had insisted on making counter-charges against the three policemen, and his solicitor was doing all he could to make the magistrate sympathetic to his cause. Lunn was asked to describe the assault on him by Wheywell, who informed the magistate that he had asked the defendant to leave the premises, such were his orders, and having had chance to leave peacefully, Wheywell had decided to throw a punch at him. This was assault on a police officer in his line of duty.

Mr Harry Morris, defending, suggested that 'what Wheywell had done to you, you paid back at 4,000 per cent?' to which Lunn replied, 'I do not see it like that. I only did my duty knowing the man as I do. No licensees in Sheffield want these men; they only serve them out of fear. We have had enough of the gangs.' Due to the state of Wheywell, and the insistence of the defence that both sides of the fracas should be answerable in court, the magistrate decided that he must follow the letter of the law, and recommend that the case be heard at the quarter sessions. There had been several witnesses who would testify on Wheywell's behalf, including, surprisingly, the pub landlord.

When the case came around, it was strikingly obvious that the charges against the policemen were nothing more than an attempt to remove them from the everyday lives of the gangs. The witnesses mentioned in the magistrates' court were hardly a trustworthy bunch, as they consisted of Harry Rippon, Peter Winsey and Henry Dale, all of them major players in the reformed Mooney Gang. The judge dismissed the case against the policemen almost immediately, stating that:

'If Wheywell had begun by striking the officer, as I believe the evidence shows, and that what the officer did was after that, believing that he was going to offer further violence, then PC Lunn acted in an entirely lawful manner, as did his colleagues.'

Wheywell, however, was not so lucky, and was handed down a sentence of three months of hard labour for assaulting a police officer in the line of duty. This was quite ironic, as had he simply taken his chances before the magistrate, it was highly likely that he would have got away with a fine or being bound over to keep the peace.

A similar tale occurred during the festive season of 1925. On Christmas Eve, a man named Thomas Windle arrived back in Sheffield, after having served nine months of hard labour for a razor attack on a rival gang member. Having been part of the younger Park Brigade crowd, Windle had returned a harder and more experienced man, and was ready to renew his ties with the gang.

However, as the Flying Squad had been formed during Windle's incarceration, they decided to pay him a visit upon his return, to let him know that the gangs were now being closely watched. D.S Robinson was more than happy to break the news, and went into the Norfolk Arms to deliver the message. He asked Windle to step outside, which irked the young gang member somewhat, and as the two men exited the pub, Windle was already launching an abusive tirade in Robinson's direction. The other three officers approached, and would later testify that Windle had thrown a punch at PC Loxley (which does not seem likely) before being 'subdued' by the Flying Squad. Things went from bad to worse for Windle, as he was handcuffed and marched to the Central Police Station, only to fall over several times during the short journey. This, the four policemen explained to the desk sergeant, was the reason for the prisoner being covered in blood and barely conscious.

Ironically, when Windle appeared before the magistrate on 28 December, he was defended by Mr Harry Morris, who was the duty solicitor. Morris had also represented Ganner Wheywell after his run in with the Flying Squad, and had already experienced the frustration of attempting to make the four men answerable for their actions. Addressing the magistrate, Morris fumed 'Look at the state of the defendant! It is a case of the Flying Squad on the warpath again.' The magistrate then asked PC Loxley if any of the defendant's injuries had been inflicted by the police, to which the giant constable replied 'No, it was from falling' to which Morris replied, 'It always is.' Having warned Morris to keep his cool and not to make allegations against the police unless he could prove them, Alderman Knowles, the presiding magistrate addressed Windle, saying, 'This is a very serious assault. We must protect our police in their onerous duties. You will be committed to four months with hard labour.'

One can only imagine that Morris was absolutely livid to have seen another client imprisoned whilst bruised and bandaged. However, the police had long been calling for the assistance of the magistrates, and it would appear that the Flying Squad were now as untouchable as the gangs had been before them.

The war against the gangs was yielding some impressive results, but there was to be a high-profile casualty along the way. After a meeting of the Watch Committee, in which the new approach to tackling organised crime was candidly discussed, it was decided that Chief Constable Hall-Dalwood was to take a leave of absence for one month. The Watch Committee refused to comment any further, apart from to confirm that Hall-Dalwood had not resigned, and had taken leave due to ill health. There would be no further information until the next Watch Committee meeting which would take place in a month's time. This would lead to several speculative stories appearing in the press.

The 1 October edition of the *Sheffield Mail* ran a story which openly suggested that several of Hall-Dalwood's colleagues had made statements to the Watch Committee, voicing their lack of confidence in his leadership, and bemoaning his lack of stomach for the new and tougher policing regime. However, having made these damning comments, the *Mail* then took every effort to distance itself from its sources. The article ended with a paragraph which can only be likened to a disclaimer; absolving itself of involvement in the details which had been printed above.

> 'The people of Sheffield will do well to discount heavily much irresponsible talk that is being circulated and to await the official statement, which will be made, no doubt, at the earliest possible moment.'

Yet, when the time came for the next monthly Watch Committee meeting, the only statement to be released was that the Chief Constable had been given a further three months of leave. A police surgeon had even been called in to produce a certificate which stated that Hall-Dalwood was 'unable to perform his duties due to ill-health' and that he required 'a period of complete rest and recuperation'. As expected by those in the know, Hall-Dalwood would never return to his office, and made the decision to resign before his three months leave of absence had ended. He made no public statement, and chose to leave the talking to those who remained in office. However, he was soon to have the opportunity to make his feelings known.

Having served in the Sheffield police force for thirteen years, the former Chief Constable was afforded every honour befitting a retiring leader. His official retirement dinner took place at the town hall on 31 March 1926, where, after being presented with an expensive radio set, Hall–Dalwood took to the stage and made the following statement:

> 'It has been my misfortune to become the victim of some insidious influence from outside, which for years has been working against me. At times, during the war (on the gangs), and since, my anxieties have been seriously increased by these disquieting and horrible elements, which rendered one's position almost intolerable;
>
> Perhaps after my twenty four years experience [as a police officer], my impression of what a chief officer of police should be may be wrong, but at any rate I knew what I wanted. I got it in efficiency. I am particularly satisfied with the results in spite of the evil attempts to undermine my authority.'

The speech was met by rapturous cheering and applause from the rank and file officers of the Sheffield police force, but not by the guests who held high office in the city. Hall–Dalwood left the stage to a verse of 'For He's a Jolly Good Fellow', and would never appear in the public eye after this point. He had earned his retirement, and was under no illusion that his bridges had been well and truly burnt.

The cryptic comments made by the former Chief Constable had succeeded, as was probably intended, in piquing the interest of the local press. Many attempts were made to entice Hall–Dalwood into an interview in which he would be given the chance to expand on his speech, but he turned down every approach; resulting in the *Sheffield Daily Telegraph* reporting:

> 'We may perhaps venture to suggest that Col Hall–Dalwood should go a little more into detail regarding the 'insidious influence from outside' which he claims had for years been working against him. It seems to us a public duty he owes to Sheffield and its citizens.
>
> 'Especially should we like to know whether the disquieting and horrible element still exists, and whether it is likely to continue to interfere with the work of the police?

It is the future that interests us more than the past, and if Col Hall-Dalwood would be a little more explicit, he might perhaps enable us to safeguard the police force against influences which he declares seriously increased his own anxieties and rendered his position almost intolerable.'

No response was ever received, but it was obvious to those who knew and had worked with Hall-Dalwood as to the identity of the 'insidious influence'. He had fallen foul of the Watch Committee, which had been waiting with bated breath ever since the Chief Constable's damning allegations against the city magistrates. He had threatened to uncover a cancer in the Sheffield legal system, and this would have proved greatly embarrassing to the city. Therefore, the new approach to policing, as set down by the Home Secretary, gave the Watch Committee an excuse to call for a new face at the head of Sheffield's struggling police force.

Chapter 12

The Captain Cometh

'It's hard to lead a cavalry charge if you think you look funny on a horse.'

Adlai Stevenson, American Politician (1900–1965)

Hall-Dalwood's successor began his duties on the worst possible day. He had taken his seat in the Chief Constable's office on the morning on which the General Strike began, a day in which every major city in the nation was expecting scenes of chaos and riotous crowds. The man who would be tasked with bringing Sheffield back to order would begin by witnessing the city at its most unruly. The strike was expected to last for a number of days, if not weeks, and on this first morning, there had already been scenes of unrest, with a non-unionist driver being attacked for delivering beer to a local pub, and several workers receiving threats and minor injuries after attempting to report for their duties at the steelworks.

Although sympathetic to the plight of the Unions, it has to be said that the majority of Sheffield's citizens were against the strike. The men needed to work in order to provide for their families, and the city as a whole had already had enough of chaos on the streets. To control the situation would take a great deal of consideration and dedication from a man who had just arrived in the city.

In order to keep control of the streets, the police had hastily organised the enrolment of a number of special constables. It was expected that a few hundred would take up the offer to receive a small stipend for assisting the police, yet, by the end of the strike which lasted for nine days, the new leader of the Sheffield police could boast over 7,000 volunteers. Many of these would stay on after the strike to assist in patrolling their city. The Special Duties Squad had taken over the majority of the seriously dangerous work, and the volunteers could safely go about their business performing routine duties and patrols, largely unhindered by the gangs who had found themselves on an increasingly short leash.

It had been just over a week since Hall-Dalwood's replacement had arrived in Sheffield, and already the fortunes of the police force were looking far rosier than they had done for many years. The new leader had the backing of the Home Secretary, the support of his city, and most importantly, a thirst for battle. By the time the strike had been ended, and the streets returned to normality, the new Chief Constable had yet even to introduce himself to the citizens of Sheffield, instead choosing to deal with the pressing issues of the city before making time for social niceties. Sheffield had suffered very little damage compared with other cities, and this was seen as testament to decisive and quick actions being taken by the new man in charge. It was not until the buses and trams began to run again and the men of the city were safe to return to work that the incumbent Chief Constable would agree to meet with the press.

Yet, there were to be no revealing interviews, no political manoeuvres, and absolutely no comment as to the barbed comments of his predecessor. Only the work history and qualifications of Captain Percy Sillitoe would be released to the city at this time; after all, in just nine days he had already proved his worth, and that was all that anybody needed to know.

The new man in office was something of an enigma. Sillitoe had been selected out of over fifty applicants, many of them far more experienced in police work and high office than the 38-year-old captain. Yet, it was the characteristics that set him apart from his rivals that enthralled the interview committee. Sillitoe was energetic, enthusiastic, and willing to accept change. It was important to the interview committee that the new Chief Constable had no ties to the local area. This was to ensure that there were no conflicts of interest, and would greatly reduce the chance of any future corruption. It was also decided that a fresh pair of eyes would be invaluable when it came to assessing the needs of the city and its police force. Sillitoe fitted the bill, as he was born in London in 1888, the year the Ripper terrified the capital. He had been a conscientious student, and was well thought of by his teachers. He was also, along with his family, an avid church-goer. He sang in the local choir and was deemed to be so talented that he was also part of the choir of St Paul's Cathedral.

Yet, despite his happiness at home, Sillitoe was keen to travel as widely as possible, and took a job with the Anglo-American Oil Company upon completing his education. This allowed him to undertake a few trips across the Atlantic, where he would keenly educate himself on the social issues and history of each place he visited. He was fascinated by the police force, having been lucky enough to observe the work of both the Metropolitan Police Force, and the New York Police Department, during his formative years. With this in mind, Sillitoe soon left his job in the oil industry and joined the police. However, it was the British South African Police force which appealed to him, and at the age of nineteen, he set sail for southern Africa. Upon arrival in Rhodesia (now Zimbabwe), Sillitoe found the job to be challenging, and the surroundings to be harsh and uncompromising. Yet, he had taken the job in search of a challenge, and grasped the opportunity with both hands, unlike many of his colleagues who chose to return to England after just a few weeks in South Africa.

After three years of dedicated service, Sillitoe was awarded the rank of Lieutenant, and was instrumental in leading his squad in their everyday duties. By the time the war broke out in 1914, he was Captain Percy Sillitoe, and as a valuable leader of men, was sent to German East Africa to command a highly trained squadron of British soldiers. Being an expert on the African terrain and also fluent in Swahili and Chinyanja, Sillitoe flourished in this new role, and trained his troop of desert soldiers admirably. In 1916, such was the reputation of the young Captain, that he was promoted to Assistant Political Officer, where his job was to visit the many tribes and communities, where he would ensure the locals of British protection, in return for their loyalty.

He returned to the South African Police after the war, but stayed less than two years, before returning home to London, where he would marry and attempt to make a life and career for himself in his homeland. However, the chance of another adventure proved to be too great, and Sillitoe, with his wife in tow, went to work for the Colonial Service in Tanganyika (now Tanzania). This was the portion of East Africa which had been taken from the Germans in their defeat, and was now in the hands of the British Empire. The job role, however, came as something of a disappointment to Sillitoe, who found that the majority of his time was taken up by administration and paperwork. Therefore, in 1922, as the official status of Tanganyika as part of the British Empire was finalised, Sillitoe took the first available chance to return to London in search of a leading role with the police. He applied for the job of Chief Constable of Hull police soon after his return, but was turned down without an interview.

Undeterred by this, Sillitoe decided to undertake a return to education, as he was aware that he lacked some crucial knowledge of the legal system. He began to study as a solicitor, and was about to take his final bar exam when a friend alerted him to a vacant Chief Constable position in Chesterfield.

This was a very much a small town opportunity, but as such, the interview panel would not be inundated with applicants, and the job itself would be perfect for Sillitoe to learn the role. With a nothing-to-lose attitude, he sent off his letter of intent, and was pleased to be invited to an interview, where the panel would be impressed by his enthusiasm and energy. He was offered the job almost immediately, and moved his family north to Derbyshire. This was as close as Sillitoe would come to Sheffield until he began his job in the city some four years later. His time in Chesterfield was quiet and a great opportunity to learn, but when an invitation came to relocate to the more prestigious police force in Beverley, Sillitoe decided that a change of scenery would be beneficial to his career.

However, he was only to stay in Beverley for around a year as he found the rural setting to be a little too tranquil for his liking, and often found himself at loggerheads with the local gentry, who would have preferred a Chief Constable who was a little more malleable when it came to bowing down to their many demands. So keen was Sillitoe to leave the largely serene and upper-class area of Beverley, that he paid particular attention to the goings-on in Sheffield, where John Hall-Dalwood seemed to have fallen foul of the powers that be. It seemed to him that the role of Chief Constable would become vacant very soon, and he spent the next three months educating himself on the city of Sheffield, and the problems it faced.

Towards the end of his career, Sillitoe would state in his autobiography that he was aware that the job in Sheffield would be an arduous one, but he was keen to recapture that sense of adventure which had recently been missing from his life. 'I feel sure,' he said, 'that whatever else I find in Sheffield, there would at least be plenty of hard work.' It was with this attitude that Sillitoe arrived at his eventual interview. He could boast only three years of experience as a Chief Constable, and was asking for the chance to lead the police in one of the nation's toughest places. Yet, his enthusiasm shone through, and in just a few weeks, it was announced that Captain Percy Sillitoe would be filling the well-worn boots of John Hall-Dalwood.

On starting his new role, Sillitoe was keen to see as many of his new charges in action as possible, and was immediately impressed with the Special Duties Squad. He had worked with such groups before in South Africa, where the most physically gifted men were often used in special units with the sole intention of quashing any signs of resistance. Ever the hands-on type of leader, Sillitoe even accompanied the squad on a few of their call outs, watching from a relatively safe distance as the gang members were unceremoniously dealt with. He was extremely impressed with what he saw, but questioned whether four men was enough for the squad, and how he would make his other officers tougher and more of a threat to the gangs. Interestingly, his approach to toughening up his police force was to remove every man from his duties for seven weeks, where each constable or detective would be trained in many kinds of hand to hand combat. The training was to be undertaken on full pay, and, he reasoned, would be of great help to every man in his everyday duties.

His choice of tutor raised a few eyebrows to begin with, as Sillitoe approached Professor Harry Hunter with his bold idea. Professor Hunter was more than happy to oversee the training, but not in the academic sense one would imagine; he was the European Ju-Jitsu champion, having trained extensively whilst living and lecturing in Japan. As successful as the Flying Squad were, Sillitoe was aware that he could not make the majority of his men into huge bare-knuckle boxers, and reasoned that the art of Ju-Jitsu would teach the men balance, awareness, and the ability to defend and restrain. He would happily leave the really rough stuff to the Flying Squad, but would rest more easily knowing that all of his charges would stand a decent chance against any thug.

As for the Flying Squad, the four founder members were bolstered by a few new recruits. These were taken from a list of individuals provided to Sillitoe by Professor Hunter, which contained the names of those who seemed to be most suitable for the task. Amongst these was PC Pat Geraghty, who did not take to martial arts, but was six feet five inches tall and had managed to defeat his tutor with nothing more than brute strength.

Although founded by his predecessor, Sillitoe took a personal pride in the Flying Squad (as even he referred to them by this point) and spent much of his time with the squad's leader, Sgt Robinson, with whom he would spend many hours discussing missions and tactics. This was mentioned in later years by Robinson himself:

'The Captain had been here two weeks when he called me into his office. He said to me "I have not met you before, but I've read a lot about you and what you have done. I want to congratulate you on the work you and your men are doing."

'He told me to carry on the good work and he would always be there to back me and my men up. He always appeared in court to stick up for his men.'

This was true, as one problem faced by the Flying Squad under Hall-Dalwood's regime, was that they often found themselves on the receiving end of allegations and ambitious defence solicitors. Hall-Dalwood had not gone to great lengths to stand up for the squad, and as such, had risked losing members of his elite team on several occasions. Sillitoe was not prepared to lose a single man to an over-officious magistrate or the word of a gang member. As such, whenever there was doubt about the way the Flying Squad had taken care of a situation, Sillitoe would personally attend the court hearing to endure that his men were afforded every bit of leeway necessary for them to perform their jobs effectively.

The new Chief Constable was prepared not only to take on the gangs, but also to ask the awkward, but necessary, questions of the local magistrates. His men could not fight the gangs without their participation, and he was more than prepared to discuss this matter publicly if need be. The pay-offs and the clandestine deals had to be eradicated.

In his quest to ensure the protection of his officers, Sillitoe also attended a number of court cases in which the Flying Squad had not been involved, but members of his police force had been attacked or threatened. Most notable was a case in which a husband and wife had been arrested for affray with another man, and had both struck a constable during their subsequent arrest. Ever the protector of his men, Sillitoe asked the magistrate if he could make a statement from the witness box, to which the magistrate, with very little choice, agreed. What followed was a plea to the courts to offer his men every protection available by ensuring that only the harshest punishments were handed out in the case of assault against a police officer:

'It is perhaps rather unusual to come to a case like this, but there have been so many cases of this kind recently that I wish to ask that in this case exemplary punishment be given to these people. There has been a series of outbreaks of hooliganism in this district and I feel that the police must be protected.

'The only way is by exemplary sentences so that other people cannot think that they can do this sort of thing. I am determined to stop this kind of thing so long as it rests in my power to do so, but it rests with the Bench whether I shall be supported or not.

There is an unruly element in this district who use filthy language, and when the police remonstrate with them attempt to take the law into their own hands.'

One can only imagine that the defendants in this case were wondering just how unlucky they could have been, as both men were handed down six month prison sentences, whilst the woman was bound over for £2. Had Sillitoe not been in the court that day, it is more than likely that all three of them would have been out of court, and in the pub, by lunchtime. Also in court that day was a reporter from the *Sheffield Mail*, who, whether by design or by happy coincidence, was able to take down Sillitoe's impromptu speech. The next morning, an article appeared in the same newspaper, which shared the Chief Constable's views, and reported his unprecedented actions to the people of the city:

> 'Every citizen of Sheffield will echo the determination of Captain Sillitoe, to put an end to the hooligan outbreaks, a recrudescence of which in the Shalesmoor quarter has been productive of several ugly affrays of late.
>
> 'We are pleased that the Chief Constable did not plead in vain to the magistrates to support him in his task by taking a serious view of a typical hooligan assault on a police officer. A sentence of six months hard labour will, no doubt, tend to cool the ardour of the amateur Apaches with a penchant for interfering with the police.
>
> 'We think we may promise in the name of the citizens that the Chief Constable will have the support of all good citizens, the Bench of magistrates, and the civic authorities in every effort to teach the volatile elements of the underworld that violence pays dividends in the form of hard labour.
>
> 'Sheffield is not Chicago. Human life and limb are not exposed to American crime risks or a percentage of those risks. Way back in Michigan our Sheffield gang affrays would seem small affairs to the gunmen and machine gun bandits. But let us take a step away from the Chicago complex.
>
> 'We would trim the nails of our comparatively mild hooligans without any municipal hysterics. Decent working folk have no time to tolerate an attempt at rule by street corner bullies.'

The article was received warmly by the people of Sheffield who were glad to see that something had been done to ensure tougher punishments for the violent elements of the city, yet also that these small-time crooks had not been afforded any sense of grandeur. One does have to wonder though, if anybody pointed out that Chicago is in Illinois, not Michigan!

Sillitoe had done a fine job of ingratiating himself within his new hometown, and had begun a journey which would see him cleaning up several cities, including an advisory role in Chicago itself. His journey would also see him working for MI5 in his later years. He wrote a fine autobiography, *Cloak without Dagger*:

'There was a typical case for instance, of a gangster named [Albert] Foster. He was a 'razor king' and carried a razor blade stuck into a piece of wood hidden up his sleeve and fixed to a piece of elastic. On the least pretext he would pluck the razor down from his sleeve and use it mercilessly.

'He had several convictions of assaulting and slashing people, and had been merely fined each time. The more convictions he got, the greater he was held in fear, and the quicker his fine was paid for him. He had developed contempt for authority which was hardly surprising.

'One night there was trouble at a licensed house in West Bar. Loxley and Lunn strode in. One of the men there was Foster, and as soon as he saw Loxley, he jumped at him with the razor flashing.

'He was promptly seized with 'reasonable force' and removed from West Bar to the police charge office, a distance of 200 yards. The desk sergeant refused to accept the charge until Foster had been treated at the infirmary. He was charged with being drunk and disorderly and assaulting PC Loxley.

'Next day I was in court. The public gallery was crowded with Mooney gangsters. As soon as the proceedings began, Foster's solicitor stood up and said he objected to the charge. He cast a significant glance at the huge PC Loxley and then down at the figure of his bandaged and cowed client in the dock;

'"I wish to have the charge amended your worship, from assaulting the police ... to one of attempted suicide."

'There was a howl of laughter in which all the gangsters in the public gallery joined, and I remember that even the magistrates permitted themselves to smile.'

Although Sillitoe would go on to be regarded as one of the most famous police officers and spy catchers in British history, and rightly so, one must also take a moment to remember that his achievements in Sheffield were largely due to the tireless groundwork already laid by his predecessor. Many would argue that the birth of the Flying Squad had come from an order which originated from high above the head of Hall-Dalwood, but it was still he who assembled the original team, and also created the battle plans for their first few jaunts into enemy territory. In short, we should remember this period in Sheffield's history as being the legacy of both men, rather than just part of the wider tale of Percy Sillitoe.

Although this sentiment is shared by a few local historians, history itself has seen to it that the man responsible for ridding the city of the gangs was Percy Sillitoe, which, to a degree, it was.

Chapter 13

Where There is Life

'How slow life is, how violent hope is.'

Guillaume Apollinaire, French Poet and Author (1880–1918)

T he Fowler brothers had not expected things to turn out like this. Whether they had stabbed Jock Plommer or not, the predicament they were currently in must have felt extremely harsh for people who had grown used to being almost immune to the law. However, be that as it may, they had been convicted of murder, and must face the consequences. The two had at least been allowed to share a cell in the condemned wing of Armley Prison. With the death sentence having been passed upon them, there were no real reasons to keep them apart. They were free to spend their days playing cards and writing letters, as there was no work detail for condemned men.

The warders of the condemned wing would later remark on how quiet the brothers had been. Wilfred never really seemed to snap out of the state of shock he had been in since his sentencing, and Lawrence seemed to be in the hold of a great brooding depression; understandably in his situation.

However, the brothers took the time to write to their family, all the while trying to put a cheery face on their predicament, and assuring their parents that they were doing everything they could to appeal the sentence. Below is a letter written by Lawrence on behalf of them both:

'Dear Mother, Dad and All

Don't take it too much to heart. We never expected this, but Fenoughty is making an appeal on our behalf. While there is life there is hope.

Bear up. There is still time for things to straighten out. We are happy and well considering the blow, and keeping in the best of spirits. If any of you want to come and visit us you must send us word. You will write to us both, as we don't go out together.

From your ever loving sons,
Lol and Wilf'

Whether or not the family ever decided to visit the brothers is unknown, but it can be surmised that they would have received very few visitors, as the prison had been warned by the courts against allowing any of their gang mates to visit; not that there were many of them left at liberty since the recent events.

Letters from other gang members were also withheld from the brothers, who received correspondence only from immediate family members and their hard-working defence team. The last days of Lawrence and Wilfred Fowler would have been incredibly lonely had they not had each other for company.

In this brutally bleak environment, the two had become pale shadows of their former selves. These were young men who had been well known on the streets of Sheffield, mostly for the wrong reasons. Yet, they had enjoyed being part of the gang, and enjoyed the money and status that came with it even more.

Lawrence was always well known for his flashy clothing. He favoured white or light-coloured suits, finely tailored, and often topped with a straw boater hat which would be tipped at a fashionable angle. He was very much the man about town, and although he was happily married, he was also something of a self-confessed ladies' man. He had a reputation for being very quick tempered, and would often change from being jovial and chatty one moment, to being angry and violent the next. He had an extremely short fuse and often had to be calmed down by other gang members when it seemed that he was about to lose his temper over something unimportant.

Wilfred was very much the opposite. He was a handsome young family man, but cared very little for clothes and women. He was a quiet man who simply wanted to fit in. Like Lawrence, he did have a terrible temper, but never really showed a contrasting jovial side. He was a young man who would do whatever he was told by the older gang members or his older brother.

The attack on Harold Liversidge which had started this whole mess had been as a result of a direct order from some older gang mates. Yet, when push literally came to shove later that night, there were none of them to be seen as he and his brother went out into the street to meet with Liversidge and Plommer. To all intents and purposes, the two seemed to have been used as pawns by the more senior gang members. They could very well have been the men who struck the fatal blows, but they would not have been carrying a bayonet without prior approval from Sam Garvin, a man who gave a lot of thought to every action he sanctioned.

As it stood, whether rightly or wrongly, the two were the sacrificial lambs to the slaughter. They had only been gang members for a relatively short time, but had found themselves as scapegoats where the gang was concerned, and ruffians to be made an example of by the legal system. Either way, they were almost certainly doomed.

To add to the sense of tragedy, Wilfred had spent his 24th birthday in his condemned cell, and had been visited by his wife and daughter. Later that day, the heavily pregnant Mrs Fowler gave birth to another daughter without her husband by her side. The new baby was brought in to see Wilfred some two weeks later, and although he was allowed to hold the child for a few moments, he broke down in tears as his visitors were told that it was time to leave. This would more than likely be the only time he would ever see his second child, and probably the last time he would see his loving wife and young daughter. Lawrence too had been visited by his own wife, but she had refused to bring their children to the prison. Due to her husband's positive disposition and empty promises, she still firmly believed that their appeal had every chance of being successful. Yet, as soon as she had left, Lawrence was forced to face reality once again, and withdrew back into this depression. It was true that there was an appeal being lodged on their behalf, but they had already been advised by their legal team that it was extremely unlikely that they would receive any kind of reprieve. However, a case had been formulated, and would be made before the high court in the next few days. This was the last roll of the dice for the Fowler brothers.

The man leading the fowler's appeal was Mr J.W. Fenoughty, the man who had long been on the payroll of Sam Garvin, and had represented the Park Brigade members in court many times. Even the four different solicitors who represented the ten men at the trial had been under the instruction of the experienced and tenacious legal mind of Mr Fenoughty. Although he did not hold out much hope for a reprieve, Fenoughty had identified a few areas which could be questioned and exploited in the interest of sparing his clients the death sentence. With a sense of urgency, he put together an appeal with a slight chance of success, but was aware that this would have to be delivered perfectly to a lenient judge in order for the sentence to be overturned. All in all, there were too many factors which were out of his control. Whether or not the appeal would be presided over by an understanding judge, whether the judge would actually pay attention to the cracks in the case, and whether the prosecution decided to challenge their evidence; all remained to be seen.

The main factors deemed to be grounds for appeal seemed quite reasonable. The trial had been fairly brutal where the brothers were concerned, as their guilt in the crime had been assumed right from the beginning. As such, the following factors were brought before the high court: that one of the brothers may have been guilty of manslaughter, rather than murder, but there had been no consideration of this point; that there had been no proven distinction between Lawrence and Wilfred Fowler, and the other men who had been sentenced for manslaughter; that the verdict was disproportionate against the weight of the evidence provided during the trial.

The Court of Criminal Appeal accepted the above reasons to challenge the sentence, possibly due to the fact that, even though the death sentence was still fairly commonplace, the law was becoming a little squeamish in actually upholding it, and the execution of two young brothers was bound to cause a national media frenzy. There were very few occasions where an appeal would not be granted when a death sentence had been handed down, but most of these were summarily dealt with, especially when the weight of the evidence was greatly against the defendant. The Fowler brothers, however, were afforded a proper chance to be defended for a second time.

For the brothers themselves, the appeal at least provided them with a small glimmer of hope, but the red tape and legal necessities in lodging the appeal meant that their stay in the condemned cell would turn out to be a long and gruelling one. They would eventually spend eight months in this wing of the prison while their lives were being fought for on the outside. Most condemned prisoners would spend just a few weeks housed in this particular wing, and the strict regime and stark nature of these particular cells must have made the brothers question, on occasion, whether the whole appeal was worth this extended incarceration with only each other, and four stone walls for company.

With only one chance to appeal the sentence, the defence counsel took their time over preparing their case, quite rightly so when lives depended on the outcome. Save for a few updates from their solicitor, Lawrence and Wilfred would be largely left to spend their days thinking about the lives they had left behind, and carrying on their bleak existence. Yet, as Lawrence had previously written to his parents; where there was life, there was hope. They did receive a few visits from immediate family members, but the sanctions placed on them having any contact with gang members was upheld for the duration of their imprisonment, which mean that the few friends the brothers had who were still at liberty were unable to write or visit. The outside world must have seemed a million miles away for these two former men-about-town.

The day of the appeal did not arrive until 18 April 1926. For the hearing, the two brothers were allowed to leave their cell, and were taken to the Court of Criminal Appeal in London by an early morning train, accompanied at all times by warders, who would be chained to them constantly throughout the journey. By this time, the previously handsome and well-dressed young men bore little resemblance to their former selves. Both appeared emaciated and drawn as they were shepherded into the especially reserved train carriage, in which they would be transported to London without even a view from the windows, which were covered by heavy blinds. There had been concerns that the remaining gang members would take the opportunity to disrupt the transportation, and possibly attempt a rescue of their former colleagues. Therefore, the train that had been selected was a slow train which set off at an ungodly hour. This was to be anything but a pleasant journey for Lawrence and Wilfred Fowler.

On arrival in the capital, the two were quickly bundled into an awaiting police vehicle and locked in. The van and driver had been borrowed for the occasion from the Metropolitan Police, which allowed the warders to remain chained to their prisoners whilst being transported from the station to the courthouse. Having been placed separately into holding cells below the court, and fed a basic breakfast of tea and bread, the brothers could do nothing more than to stare at a different collection of stone walls until the time came for them to be brought through the corridors and up the steps into the dock. The next few important hours would decide whether they would live or die.

All in all, it had already been a gruelling day, and the proceedings had not yet even begun. However, it can be imagined that not many people would have had any sympathy for the Fowler brothers, least of all the wife and children of Jock Plommer.

Leading the appeal was Mr G.H.B. Streatfield, who had represented the brothers in their original trial, and who was under the direction of Mr Fenoughty as he had been for the duration of the case. Measuring his words carefully and taking all of the time allowed to him, Mr Streatfield began the day by describing to the court the events of the original trial, and laying out his objections to the handling of his clients. The main focus of the defence had been of the judge himself, Mr Justice Findlay, who, Mr Streatfeld argued, had been instrumental in allowing misdirection and non-direction of the jury during the original trial. There were several reasons for their concern, which would all be laid out before the presiding judge before the day was out.

Streatfield also made it clear that he was in no way disputing that the Fowler brothers should not be severely punished for their actions on the night in question. They admitted to have being involved on the attack on Jock Plommer, and would also be happy to confirm that they had lied repeatedly in court. The main aim of the appeal, he admitted, was for the judge to re-examine the case, and to amend the charge of murder handed to the brothers, to a lesser charge of manslaughter. They had been part of a mob attack, and should be punished in the same way as the other members of that mob. There was no definitive evidence to suggest that they had inflicted the fatal wounds to the victim.

The main error made by Mr Justice Findlay, Streatfield suggested, was during his long and drawn out summing up, where he had deliberately grouped defendants together in his speech to the jury. He had questioned the intent of Wills, Stewart and Harker in their actions, but had then referred to the Fowlers in a way which suggested that they were guilty of more serious offences. If the judge had believed one of the brothers to be guilty of inflicting the fatal wounds, he should have made this clear, rather than grouping the two together for his own convenience. He had made no differentiation in the eye witness statements against each man, and had also not made mention of their differing motives.

The defence counsel believed this to have had an adverse effect on the minds of the jury, who now seemed to be instructed to charge the brothers as if they were one man. Therefore, if one was guilty, both must be guilty by default. The question of which man had been responsible for the stab wounds should have been the most important decision for the jury. If the identity of the killer had been addressed, it would have been clear to the jury that both men could not possibly have been guilty of inflicting the stab wounds to the victim, and at least one of them would have been found guilty of manslaughter. The judge had made a serious error in convincing the jury that they were not to differentiate between Lawrence and Wilfred Fowler in their deliberations.

The defence also argued that during the attack on Plommer, the part played by the men in the dock was no different from the actions of the men found guilty of manslaughter. All had eventually admitted to being in possession of weapons during the attack, and the only differentiation between them all was that a witness described seeing one of them holding a bayonet at some point.

All in all, Mr Streatfield argued that there had been considerably less evidence against his clients than there had been against the other men. Only a few mentions of Lawrence Fowler making a stabbing motion with an unidentified item, and Wilfred Fowler being accused of putting a bayonet into a case by just one witness, had been enough for Mr Justice Findlay to assume their guilt.

For all of the eye witness accounts and investigation into what took place that night, it had still never been proven that either of the brothers had used the bayonet against the victim. Not one witness could claim to have seen this, and not one of the other defendants had mentioned anything about this in their own defence. It would have been entirely expected, he added, that at least one of the men who also had the threat of the black cap hanging over them, would have informed the court if they knew who had inflicted the blows. It was one thing to uphold the code of the criminal, but entirely another to keep silent when the possibility of the noose was forthcoming. These were hardened criminals and dedicated gang members, but surely none of them would have risked execution if they had known who the real culprit was. It would have been entirely rational, Streatfield argued, that at least one of them would have given up the confidence of a friend in order to save their own life.

With this, the defence had listed their every objection to the sentences handed down, and could only wait until the presiding judge, Lord Chief Justice Swift, had taken to time to consider their arguments. This was to be an agonising wait for all involved, especially Lawrence and Wilfred Fowler, who were returned to their cells whilst their lives were being decided.

The wait had been almost intolerable, but things were about to get a whole lot worse for the Fowler brothers. Having been escorted back to the dock, the two were told to stand as the judge re-entered the courtroom, only to waste no time in informing them that he had not seen fit to overturn their sentences. Aware that the defendants had already spent months in the condemned wing, and had spent an uncomfortable day in the cells, Lord Chief Justice Swift had decided to deliver the earth-shattering decision as quickly as possible, and announced that he would discuss the finer points with the defence counsel when the condemned men had been taken back down below.

The judge had reasoned that the original jury had understandably found the brothers guilty of murder, as a large number of the testimonies heard during the trial had pointed the finger at them, and that both had motive following the incidents of the previous night. In his opinion, the fatal blow was dealt by one of them, and having arrived armed with such a weapon, were both equally guilty. Swift did concede that he may have been persuaded, had he been the trial judge, to find more of the men guilty of murder, but this, he reasoned, bore no relevance on the sentences handed down to the brothers. 'Just because more men could have been hanged, does not mean that you should not be,' he informed the brothers.

In defence of Mr Justice Findlay, Swift declared that he saw no reason why the summing up of the case should be criticised. Findlay had done a fine job in officiating over a case which involved so many defendants and so many versions of events. There had simply been no other way to deal with the case.

Reaffirming the sentence passed against the Fowlers, Swift stated that it was little wonder that the jury found them guilty of murder, given the number of corroborating eyewitness statements, and a motive set them apart from the other men at the trial. Lawrence Fowler slumped back into his chair, only to be dragged to his feet by the warders, whilst Wilfred yelled, 'Others are guilty as well!' before being taken back to the cells.

With the prisoners having been removed from the dock, Swift was more than willing to explain his decision in more detail to the defence counsel. He was aware that there had been a lack of concrete evidence against them, but the sheer amount of circumstantial evidence against them was damning in the extreme. Also, having carefully considered the appeal, he could find absolutely no evidence that the original trial had not been conducted to the very letter of the law, and although singling out two of ten men to receive the death penalty may seem harsh, he confided that he would have done exactly the same had he been the presiding judge at the time of sentencing. There were two main reasons, he added, that the brothers had been singled out. Firstly, not one witness had claimed to have seen any of the other men either making a stabbing motion, or in possession of the murder weapon, and secondly, that the brothers themselves, during their own testimonies, failed to implicate any of the other defendants, even going as far as to claiming they had never met the men before. In doing the latter, Lawrence and Wilfred Fowler had very much signed their own death warrant. They had 'practically invited the jury to find only themselves guilty of murder'. Whether convinced that the evidence against them was weak, or foolishly sticking to the unwritten criminal's code, the brothers had given the court an opportunity to make an example of them.

The decision had been made, and Lord Chief Justice Swift had absolutely no qualms in sending the two young men to their deaths. A man had been brutally attacked and murdered in the street, and those responsible must face the proper punishment for each part played in the crime.

While Mr Streatfield and his team seem to have done everything they could to argue the case of their clients, there are a few aspects of the case which had not been investigated. As Bean says:

> 'Surprisingly, Mr Streatfield does not appear to have raised the matter of the missing murder weapon, allegedly the bayonet stated by witnesses to have been in the Fowler's possession. Despite an intensive search of the Attercliffe district, including the Fire Brigade using an electro-magnet to scan the River Don from a rowing boat, the weapon which killed William [Jock] Plommer was never found.
>
> 'It is surprising that a greater importance was not attached to this by the defence at the trial for if, between the incident with Plommer and their confrontation with PC Hogan on the chip shop steps, the Fowlers had the opportunity to dispose of a bayonet, a question that must be asked is why they had not also disposed of the poker and razor found on them by the police officer?
>
> 'Evidently, another person present at the scene of the affray removed the weapon, as it is extremely doubtful that the Fowlers could have disposed of it in a way that it would never be found, between Norfolk Bridge and the chip shop steps in Princess Street – a distance of barely fifty yards – with all eyes on them.
>
> 'None of the witnesses who identified Lawrence and Wilfred Fowler as being in possession of the bayonet claimed to have seen them dispose of it, so what became of it?
>
> 'The defence seem to have allowed its disappearance to remain a mystery. Had the question been explored, however, perhaps the Fowler's explanation for the poker and razor – that they took them from Plommer – might have been given greater credibility.'

The eye witness who claimed to have seen Wilfred Fowler putting the weapon into a case raises another important point; why someone who was about to dispose of a murder weapon bother to put it back into a case? This is just part of the eyewitness statement of one witness, who could have been mistaken about what they had seen. However, as this was the factor which largely contributed to Wilfred Fowler being convicted of murder, one would hope that the witness was absolutely certain of what they had seen. Perhaps the weapon had been put back in the case in order to conceal it on their getaway, but the facts do state that the weapon must have been disposed of very quickly, so surely it would have been quicker and easier to simply make a getaway without pausing to undo the fastenings on the box, place the bayonet inside, then do the fastenings up again before making a run for it?

Whatever actually happened with the weapon, and whether it was placed back into its case or not, is just another unanswered question in the grand scheme of things. This is a case full of holes and missing information; and it would appear that we will never know the exact story of what happened in Princess Street that night.

Chapter 14

Two Days, Two Brothers

'The love of a man for a woman waxes and wanes like the moon, but the love of brother for brother is steadfast as the stars and endures like the word of the prophet.'

P.C. Wren, British Author (1875–1941)

Just minutes after the first reporter to have spent the day in London for the appeal had sent word of the outcome by telephone to his office, the news of the Fowler's failure in avoiding execution was spreading across Sheffield like wildfire. This was the biggest news story of the year.

There was much rejoicing across the city, as the men who had personified the gang culture which had for so long held their city hostage were to swing for their crimes. This jubilant mood, however, angered those that remained members of the largely defunct Park Brigade, as did the outcome of the appeal itself.

The police were placed on high alert, as revenge attacks were expected to take place over the coming days, and the Special Duties Squad had their work cut out with keeping tabs on as many known gang members as they could. As strange as it seemed, the end of an era was to be preceded by a brief return to the old days. But, apart from a few arrests made for fairly innocuous incidents of affray and being drunk and disorderly, the trouble expected by the police never really materialised. The police were kept out on the streets in force, but were largely tasked with keeping an eye out for trouble, rather than having to deal with it. This may have been due to the remaining gang members being acutely aware that the spotlight was firmly upon them these days, even more so with the news which had arrived from London. However, the defeat of their former gang mates in court could not be ignored, so a decision was made by an unknown person to make their point in a quiet, yet threatening, manner.

The victim was the unfortunate widow of Jock Plommer, who awoke the day after the appeal to find an anonymous letter on her doormat. The note was handwritten in barely legible scrawl, but the intentions of the contents were plain enough to see. This was a warning, and had no doubt been delivered courtesy of the remnants of the Park Brigade. In the note, Mrs Plommer had been accused of having 'sworn the Fowlers lives away' and asking if she was ready to 'meet her doom' as she was soon to be 'done in'. The letter was suspected to be from one of the men who had been acquitted during the murder trial, or had at the very least been in the public gallery, as it made more than one reference to Plommer having been in possession of a poker when he approached the gang. There were also a number of references made to 'T and D', who the investigating detectives believed to be Thompson and Day, friends of Jock Plommer, and associates of the former Mooney Gang. Both men had given statements during the trial as to the good character of their deceased friend, and of the appalling character of Sam Garvin, a man with whom both had crossed paths several times. The author of the letter claimed that they would be coming for Mrs Plommer as soon as they 'had done T and D in', and happily proclaimed that they would 'swing like Kings' for all three of them. Unsurprisingly, the police were called immediately, and Mrs Plommer and her children were placed under police protection.

Mrs Plommer wasn't the only unwilling recipient of an unwanted letter. Wilfred Fowler's wife had also received a note in the post. The author of the note was obviously barely literate, as among the profanity and threats, the content seemed to be somewhat friendly, as if it was written by somebody acting on her behalf, and was sharing his intentions of revenge. The note finished 'might write later i hear anything'. Other recipients of threatening letters were those who had provided the damning eyewitness accounts during the trial, and had been brave enough to take the stand in person. Each woke to find a hastily scribbled note marked for their attention at some time over the following week.

Some of the threats were delivered in person, usually by junior members of the Park Brigade, who approached Harold Liversidge, Harry Rippon, and Spud Murphy individually, delivering a message from the gang which stated in no uncertain terms that revenge would be taken against them for their parts in testifying against the ten members of the Park Brigade. The messenger had obviously underestimated the character of Spud Murphy, who reportedly listened to the warning in silence, before beating seven bells out of the young man, and then proceeded to chase him for several hundred yards before finally returning back to his local pub for a much-needed pint.

Murphy managed to escape any revenge attacks regarding this incident, as he, as a leading gang member, was almost always under the watchful eyes of the Flying Squad (who seem not to have been around when he gave the Park Brigade messenger a good hiding!) which in this case, was an unexpected blessing. Thompson and Day, like Mrs Plommer, had also been placed under police protection, along with their families since the arrival of the threatening letter. As such, it would appear that the targets of the Park Brigade were all out of reach for the moment, and the Flying Squad had continued to perform their duties admirably.

All that was left for the gang members was to wait and see if the one action still available to the Fowler brothers would be allowed; an appeal to the Home Secretary himself to petition the King for a pardon. However, this was as unlikely as Sam Garvin and George Mooney enjoying a quiet pint together.

On 20 August 1926, the Fowlers were granted a prolonged visit with four family members. Although it was still possible to for them receive a Royal reprieve, the prison staff had decided to allow them the few privileges afforded to condemned prisoners before the final nail in their coffin was hammered into place. Mr and Mrs Fowler, along with two of their daughters visited their boys in Armley still clinging to a tiny shred of hope. Lawrence and Wilfred were two of nine children, but they had often been the main earners in the family (usually by questionable means), and were much loved by the rest of the Fowler clan. This was to be a difficult visit, but one that the condemned men managed to brighten with a show of stoicism. Despite knowing that their final appeal to the Home Secretary would most likely be refused or ignored, they allowed their family to keep their faith in this tiny chance of a reprieve. Having assured their visitors that every effort had been taken to show their case in the best possible light to the Home Secretary, the subject was then avoided for the rest of the visit.

Mr and Mrs Fowler had been victims of much abuse over the past months, bearing the brunt of the city's feelings towards their sons, yet, this ordeal had not diminished any of the love they held for Lawrence and Wilfred, and the next three hours were spent talking, praying, and even singing the odd music hall song. The mood changed almost immediately as the family were told that the visit was over. Without the Royal reprieve, the only visit the boys could look forward to was from their own wives and children on the day of their executions. It was a tearful farewell, as it was accepted but unspoken, that this would be the last time the family would ever see their beloved boys.

Three days later, the all-important letter was sent by Mr Fenoughty to the Home Office. Unbeknown to the prisoners, the case for Wilfred Fowler had been entirely abandoned. He had been in possession of the weapon at some point according to a witness, had the strongest motive for the murder, and at the time of his arrest,had a wound to his finger which was conducive to that which could have been caused by mishandling the murder weapon. The letter was purely sent for the benefit of Lawrence Fowler, who, despite having been witnesses making stabbing motions, had not been seen with any kind of bladed weapon, and had not made the direct threats to Jock Plommer as his brother had done. Yet, this seemed nothing more than a desperate last shot at saving one out of two clients.

Things seemed especially futile, as the Home Secretary, Sir William Joynson-Hicks, had been the very man who demanded the formation of the Special Duties Squad, and had promised the Sheffield police force every assistance in ridding the city of the gangs. If there was one man in the country who was going to be unmoved by the request, it was Joynson-Hicks.

After receiving no reply, Fenoughty sent another letter two days later. This time he did receive a response, but it was not from Joynson-Hicks, it was from his Under Secretary. It was clear that the Home Secretary had not even given the appeal even a cursory glance, and had left the correspondence for his junior colleague to deal with.

This abrupt letter was received by Mr Fenoughty:

> 'Sir,
>
> With reference to your letters of the 23rd and 25th on behalf of Lawrence Fowler, now under sentence of death, I am directed by the Secretary of State to inform you that he has given careful consideration to all the circumstances of the case, and I am to express to you his regret that he has failed to discover any grounds which would justify him in advising his Majesty to interfere with the due course of the law.'

Without mentioning that Wilfred had been doomed from the outset, Mr Fenoughty visited the brothers in prison, and delivered the news in person. It was met with quiet acceptance, as both had been pre-warned that there was more chance of them *becoming* King, than of being pardoned by the King in this case. As such, all that was left for Lawrence and Wilfred Fowler was to make their peace with the world, and say their last goodbyes to their wives and children. They had been held in Armley for a long time, and the prison governor would waste no time in carrying out their executions.

On 2 September, just two days after receiving the letter from the Home Office, a notice of execution was placed outside the gates of Armley prison, stating that Wilfred Fowler was to be executed the next day, and Lawrence Fowler on the following day. The executioner was to be the revered Thomas Pierrepoint.

Thomas Pierrepoint was the second man of the family to practise the unusual profession of Licenced Executioners. He was preceded by his brother, Henry, with whom Thomas would learn the trade, and followed by his nephew, Albert, who would begin his career as Thomas' assistant. Thomas was actually the older of the Pierrepoint brothers, and had followed his father into working as a quarryman. However, from the moment his younger brother had been accepted as a Licenced Executioner (after inundating the Home Office with letters offering his service), Thomas was persuaded to join Henry in his macabre profession.

Unlike Henry, Thomas had not offered his services due to wanting to provide the most humane possible service to his convicts; he had been enticed entirely by the money. During his early manhood, Thomas was reportedly making additional income as an illegal bookmaker, but decided that money which he could make by legitimate means would be a far safer option. Despite his reasons for taking up the trade, there can be absolutely no doubt that Thomas Pierrepoint was an extremely conscientious and professional man. He and his brother were the most sought-after hangmen in the country, and would also be commissioned to carry out their work in Ireland, Gibraltar, and even further afield.

In 1912, just six years after his first execution, Thomas was entrusted with the hanging one of the most notorious killers of the decade, the poisoner Frederick Seddon, who had been executed for the murder of his lodger, Elizabeth Barrow, for his own financial gain. However, it would not be until the memoirs of his nephew were released many years later, that the work of Thomas and his brother would be known to the wider world. It was expected of these professional men that they never speak publicly about their experiences, and that all contact with the press be avoided. Therefore, the hangmen would never feature in the news, or be recognised in the street. This was simply a service they provided for an extra income whenever they were called upon.

By the time Wilfred Fowler received his last prison visit, Pierrepoint would have already been in Leeds in preparation for the executions. On hearing the news of his execution, the following day, Wilfred's wife and children had been allowed to visit him after setting out immediately from Sheffield. Since her last visit, Mrs Fowler was shocked to see the further change in her husband; he was more emaciated than before, and looked like a man who bore the weight of the world on his shoulders. These were to be their last moments together, and she had brought their two daughters, one of whom Wilfred had only seen once, to say goodbye to their father.

Upon leaving the prison gates, Mrs Fowler was approached by a *Sheffield Mail* reporter, who asked her how her husband was. She confirmed that he was frail and weak. 'My little daughter climbed on his back,' she said, 'but he was unable to bear her weight for very long. He told me to be brave, and to try to forget.' Her words appeared in the evening edition of the *Mail*, and accompanied a story in which details of Fowler's last evening were reported. It was confirmed that Fowler would be allowed to smoke, eat and drink as much as he liked, and would be allowed anything he requested within reason. Three warders would share this final evening in the cell with him. He would have been separated from his brother earlier that day, and taken to a holding cell which was exclusively used for those about to be executed. This was a more comfortable environment than his previous cell, but he would not be a resident for very much longer.

At 8 the following morning, Wilfred Fowler was roused from his bed, and was instructed to wash and dress. He was then offered a short visit from a vicar, which he refused. At 8.50, he was taken from his cell and made the short walk in the morning chill to the scaffold, whilst flanked on both sides by prison warders.

Wilfred was to be executed at the same time as another prisoner, a Rotherham ironworker, Alfred Bostock, who had been convicted of murdering his girlfriend in a jealous rage. This had led to a number of questions from those who attended, namely, if two men were to be executed together, why not Wilfred and Lawrence? It was suggested that the decision had come right from the top, and that the Home Secretary, Mr Joynson-Hicks, had refused to allow the brothers to be hanged together, as he believed that two separate executions would send a more powerful message to those who flaunted the law as part of a gang. If this was the case, then it would appear that very little consideration had been made for the Fowler family, who would wake up on two consecutive mornings knowing that one of their number would be dead by 9.01am. It was also difficult for Lawrence Fowler, who would spend his last day on earth mourning the death of his younger brother.

The executions were to take place in an outside shed, normally used as a garage for the prison van. This was due to a few problems during the last hanging at the prison, when a reporter had managed to scale a wall and take photographs of the execution. No such chances would be taken on this occasion.

By the time 9 o'clock arrived, a large crowd had gathered outside the prison gates. Many had travelled from Sheffield, and were glad to see the back of the young gang member. There was also a number of plain clothed policemen stationed amidst the crowd to ensure that none of the remaining gang members had taken the opportunity to cause trouble. There was a sense of confusion as the clock failed to strike the hour at 9, but just fifteen minutes later, the official notice of execution was posted outside the prison. Presumably, the lack of the hour chime was some small mark of respect to Lawrence Fowler, who would have been languishing in his cell while his brother swung on the end of a rope. In fact, Lawrence was well aware of the time, and collapsed in his cell as his brother breathed his last. He sobbed hysterically for a number of hours, before spending the rest of the day almost senseless in his grief. It had been a cruel tactic to separate the brothers for the last days of their lives, and even the warders passed on their sympathy to the condemned man.

Unbeknown to Lawrence, when refusing the chance to speak with the vicar, Wilfred had actually requested a piece of paper and a pencil with which he had written a confession to the crime. This also (whether truthfully or not) completely exonerated his brother, who Wilfred claimed to have been guilty of nothing more than assault. Having been informed of this, Mr Fenoughty took this final chance to make contact with the Home Secretary once more, and undertook a long and frustrating telephone correspondence with the Home Office. However, by the time the information reached the desk of Joynson-Hicks, it was summarily brushed aside. 'There has been nothing to justify interference with the carrying out of the sentence,' he said in reply to Mr Fenoughty, therefore sending the second brother to the scaffold as the first had gone just hours before. Every means of salvation had now failed for Lawrence Fowler, and his brother's well-meaning confession had been in vain.

The next morning, after refusing all food and drink the night before, Lawrence Fowler was escorted to the scaffold, as his brother had been just twenty-four hours before. This time, the bell did toll, and all present bowed their heads. The official notice of execution was posted outside the prison gates at 9.10am.

Chapter 15

The Storm before the Calm

'War is only a cowardly escape from the problems of peace.'

Thomas Mann, German Novelist (1875–1955)

All had been relatively quiet in Sheffield since the executions of the Fowler brothers, yet this had been largely due to a lack of leading gang members on the streets, as many of them had found themselves on the receiving end of prison sentences, either in the Princess Street attack, or for other crimes of violence. Even George Mooney, who had been back in Sheffield for some time, but had chosen to stay away from the gang life, had found himself receiving a prison sentence for a fairly innocuous non-gang related fight; such was his reputation that still caused fear across the city at the very mention of his name. The courts were taking no chances now, and any opportunity to lock up George Mooney would be taken.

However, by early 1927, many of the old gangsters had been released from their sentences, most notably Mooney, and Sam Garvin, who had served his time for the other assault committed on the night of the Princess Street murder. The kindling was dry, and the wind was right for an explosive event; all that was required was a spark.

The landlord of the Raven Tavern in Fitzwilliam Street was something of a chancer. Harvey Flood liked to bolster his income as a publican by running a side business as an unlicenced boxing promoter. As such, Flood had welcomed the news that both Mooney and Garvin were now back in the city.

He had hatched a plan in which he would offer a £100 purse for the winner of a boxing match between the two, and suggested that the rival gang lords could use the fight as an opportunity to settle the gang war once and for all; the winner would be £100 richer, and would hold the bragging rights over which gang eventually won the war of Sheffield. Word was sent out of this offer, and the streets were awash with excitement as false rumours emerged that both men had agreed to the fight. In reality, both had completely ignored the challenge. And neither wanted to draw any unnecessary attention upon themselves having only just been released from prison. That aside, Mooney was 37 years old, and was considerably out of shape. He had not been involved in the gang war for quite some time, and his basic instincts had softened somewhat. Garvin was 48 years old, and was not a man who liked to put himself in the firing line. Therefore, it was incredibly unlikely that this spectacle would ever occur.

With all of this in mind, it seems bizarre that the first time Mooney and Garvin would lay eyes upon each other for a matter of years would be in the pub owned by Harvey Flood. This had been nothing to do with the proposed boxing match, and simply occurred because both men fancied a drink in the Raven on the same evening.

On the evening of 28 February, George Mooney, Ganner Wheywell and Spud Murphy entered the pub with the intention of having a few quiet drinks and a catch up about the old days. Murphy was still living the gang lifestyle, but Mooney and Wheywell had both since decided to set themselves on the path to an honest life. But, if there was one thing likely to raise the animal instincts in Mooney and Wheywell, it would be catching sight of Sam Garvin, the man who took the Sky Ring away from the Mooney Gang; and on this evening, that is exactly what happened.

Sam and Bob Garvin, who had both served time for the assault upon Harry Rippon, had been in the Raven for quite some time, playing draughts and having a quiet drink, when the former members of the Mooney Gang walked in. Without a second's hesitation, the three men, led by George Mooney as in the old days, walked across to the Garvin's table and renewed their acquaintance. Ganner Wheywell was less than friendly in his approach, as he suggested to Mooney and Murphy that perhaps they should 'begin the evening by cutting their heads off'. This immediately led to a standoff, in which the draughts board was sent flying and the table overturned. Obviously, Harvey Flood did not want this particular boxing match to take place in his beloved pub, as he had called the police the moment the three men arrived.

The heated argument had turned into pushing and shoving by the time the police arrived, and a fight could only have been moments away. Wheywell made another threat, that he would shoot both of the brothers, before shouting at Sam Garvin, 'You got those two lads hung! The coppers might have been tricked, but we'll get you yet!' As the taproom began to fill with police officers, the three decided that they should leave before they spent a night in the cells. As it would turn out, all three would be arrested later that night anyway, as their behaviour was not to improve for the rest of the night. As they left, one of the men, believed to have been Wheywell, threw an ashtray through the window, covering the taproom in shattered glass.

It would seem that, at this point, Mooney and Murphy advised the incandescent Wheywell to go home before he found himself in any more trouble, and they would probably end up wishing they had joined him, as they found more trouble in the next pub they arrived at; the Royal Hotel in West Bar.

The constables who had attended the Raven wasted no time in letting the Flying Squad know that the gang members were causing scenes, and before Mooney and Murphy had even finished their first pint in the Royal, the evening crowd was parted by Sgt Robinson, PC Loxley, and PC Lunn. It would seem that the two men would not be staying in the Royal for very long either. The three men of the Flying Squad told Mooney and Murphy that the landlord had objected to their being in his establishment, and asked them to leave without a fuss. Although Murphy had already had previous experience of the Flying Squad, he was well known to have a very impulsive nature, and as such, took great delight in telling the Flying Squad where they could put their polite request.

Within seconds, Spud Murphy was flying through the night air, landing with a thud in the gutter outside the pub. Loxley and Lunn had made short work of helping him to leave the establishment. However, in an unnecessary coup de grace, his night was made even worse when he tried to get back on his feet, and he was floored once more by an almighty punch from Sgt Robinson. Having taken in this taster of what the Flying Squad was capable of; Mooney wisely chose to walk out of the pub without uttering a word. Yet, as he exited via the front door, he was also subjected to a brutal blow from Sgt Robinson, who then told Mooney that he had been waiting for a chance to meet him, and warned him that he should never let any of the Flying Squad see him causing trouble again.

Both men were frogmarched to the West Bar police station, during which time, as was customary, both men 'fell down' several times. For the umpteenth time, the Desk Sergeant sighed and called for a doctor to clean his prisoners up before they could be safely admitted to their cells for the night. Both men would appear before the magistrate in the morning. Regarding the trouble which took place in the Raven, Mooney and Murphy were both fined a reasonable £1 each for their part in the ugly scenes and damage to the window. Wheywell, however, had been called for that night by the police, and again that morning, but did not appear. A warrant was placed for his arrest.

After receiving their punishment, Mooney and Murphy were told to stay in the dock, as there was a further matter to attend to. They were then informed that they were both being charged with an assault outside the Royal Hotel later on the previous evening. The supposed victim was revealed to be the Flying Squad's own Sgt Robinson! The two defendants were given time to confer with their solicitor, Mr L.H. Brittain, at which time they told the story as it had actually occurred. Brittain was about to become another defence solicitor who had the unenviable task of trying to make a counter charge of assault against the Flying Squad.

The prosecutor, Mr G.H. Banwell, began the proceedings by reading out the statement of events as given by the Flying Squad, which stated that both men had become physically violent after being politely asked to leave the premises. Murphy especially had been 'like a madman' as he threw a number of blows and kicks against the police. Mooney, who had a number of cuts and bruises to his head, had also thrown at least one punch, according to the testimony, and had to be roughly subdued, which accounted for the wounds to his head; that and him falling over several times on the way to the police station.

Captain Sillitoe had not attended court on this occasion, but had ensured that his Flying Squad receive every bit of protection they deserved. As such, even the public who sat in the gallery could see exactly where this was going, and that perhaps, the goings-on of the previous night were not quite as the policemen had recalled.

Mr Brittain was livid that such obvious fabrications were so readily accepted by the magistrate, and spoke out in the courtroom to register his disgust at the way his clients had been treated. His comments were inflammatory and the result of a great deal of frustration, but were, nonetheless, true:

> 'I put it to you that in Sheffield it is a case of give a dog a bad name and hang, draw and quarter him, and that you are hounding these men from place to place, and out of Sheffield if need be.

At one time, Sheffield was notorious for its gangs, but now it is more notorious for its organised gangs of police, who chase these men from one licensed premises to another, and will not let them behave themselves when they want to.'

As impassioned as these words were, they had fallen upon deaf ears, and the magistrate had no problem in deciding who to believe (or who he had been told to believe). Therefore, for being thrown out of a pub and receiving a beating, Mooney and Murphy were both sentenced to two months imprisonment.

The imprisonment of Mooney and Murphy brought with it an abrupt end to most of the gang related problems in the city. The number of violent crimes fell drastically from this point onwards, and the attendances at the illegal gambling dens began to dwindle more and more each passing day.

The reason for the lack of gang activity was simply that there was no getting away with it any more. The arrival of the Flying Squad and their strong-arm tactics had been bad enough, but now that the police also had the magistrates firmly on their side, there was just no way of taking a chance in either the streets, or the courtroom. It was a little hard for the citizens of Sheffield to stomach the selective deafness which now existed between the police and the courts, but the vast majority of them would have agreed that it was all for the greater good. The honest folk could now happily go about their business without fear of the gangs for the first time in almost a decade.

Having served his short sentence and returning to his home in Rose Street, Mooney went back to his life on the straight and narrow. He had been away from the gang life for a decent period of time before that one night out with Wheywell and Murphy, and had developed a sense of content from living the quiet life. Garvin also quit the gang life, dissolving what remained of the Park Brigade, and concentrating on his own nefarious schemes. For the next few years he found himself back in court on a few occasions, but most of these appearances were due to being drunk and disorderly, and for running his own small gambling den. The Sky Ring had been abandoned along with the gang.

Ironically, both men would see each other on a regular basis, as they both had stands in the bookmakers' area of the Owlerton racetrack. Yet, there were never any reports made of trouble between the two, who went by the pseudonyms of Captain Mee (Garvin) and George Barratt (Mooney). Garvin continued to spend his time walking the line between legal and illegal activities, and it was often suspected that he was in charge of a gang of pickpockets whom he employed to travel around the racetracks in order to relieve the punters of any cash of valuables they could lay their hands on. This rumour stayed with Garvin until his death in the 1950s. Mooney continued to keep out of trouble, and would eventually be one of the most respected bookmakers in the city. He spent as much time as possible with his family, and enjoyed a drink with old friends, most of whom had also given up the gang life. George Mooney died in 1961.

The Flying Squad was disbanded in 1928, as there no longer seemed to be a need for their particular skills. One by one, the men retired with a number of thrilling stories to tell. Upon his own retirement, Walter Loxley gave an interview with the *Sheffield Telegraph*, in which he was asked what had happened to the men he had been employed to hunt down. 'Eighty percent of those boys are now going about their business in the proper way,' he said, 'but we had some very interesting times, one way or another.'

Many people will be aware of the future that lay in front of Captain Percy Sillitoe. He left the Sheffield police in 1931, having been headhunted to take over as Chief Constable of Glasgow police, who had long since been fighting their own war on gang crime. So successful was he that he was awarded a CBE for his work, and was transferred back to his native south of England to perform a similar role for the Kent police.

By the time he was awarded his most famous role, as Director General of MI5, he was Sir Percy Sillitoe, having been knighted for his part in ridding three major areas of the country of their gang problems. The man who became known as 'the gang buster' died in 1962.

What became of Jock Plommer's family is unknown, but one would hope that they found some comfort in the fact that it was his death that would ultimately lead to a city free from violent intimidation. He had stood up to the gangs, and had ultimately defeated them by laying his precious life on the line.

Postscript

Heroes and Hooligans

'So long as men worship the Caesars and Napoleons, Caesars and Napoleons
will duly rise and make them miserable.

Aldous Huxley, British Writer (1894–1963)

Walkley, Sheffield, 22 July 2017.

In researching this book, I came across an abundance of online discussion
as to the Mooney gang in particular, and was immediately taken aback by
just how fresh these dark days seem to be in the memories of the more
senior Sheffielders. Many of these folk had been told of George Mooney
and his antics by their own parents, but despite being aware of his existence,
knew very little in regards to the real story behind his time as a gang boss.

The reluctance of Mooney's name to disappear from local folklore is
quite probably due to the fact that he remained in Sheffield for decades after
the gang wars had died down, and became a (reasonably) law abiding citizen.

Sam Garvin, however, is not a name that people recognise, although his
reign of violence lasted longer than that of Mooney, and bore far more serious
consequences. This may be due to his involvement being overshadowed by
the execution of Lawrence and Wilfred Fowler, but does suggest that he
came off somewhat lightly in terms of historical infamy.

As with most historical subjects, the villains often become folk heroes
somewhere along the passage of time; a phenomenon I regularly came across
whilst researching my first book on Charlie Peace. There are hundreds of
people in Sheffield who claim to be related to George Mooney (some in
more tenuous ways than others), but I did not come across one person who
admitted to being related to Sam Garvin or the Fowler brothers.

However, the saddest fact to become apparent during my research was
that barely anybody was aware of Jock Plommer, the man whose sad and
unnecessary death provided the main event of the Sheffield gang wars. Jock
is undoubtedly the hero of the story, along with the countless thousands
that returned from war and went back to earning an honest living in a harsh

and difficult social climate. He is also the victim, along with the women who found themselves alone after the untimely death of the husbands, and were forced to pay the gangs for protection.

I am acutely aware that very few women feature in this book, and for this I make no apology. To all ends and purposes, this is a tale of cowardice and violence, and apart from one woman who went berserk with a potato masher, the women of the steel city were the ones who remained calm and composed throughout this whole tawdry affair.

The gangs were an unwanted minority amidst a city of heroes, and it is the resilience and fortitude of the Sheffield residents which deserves to be remembered, and I hope that I have made this clear throughout the book.

As there is no statue to Jock Plommer, and no street named in his honour, I have no hesitation in dedicating this book to his memory. I tried to find his headstone in the huge Burngreave Cemetery, but chose to do this on a baking hot day, and with absolutely no idea of where to start looking. Therefore, I never found him; but I hope he would have appreciated the effort.

Finally, I'd like to thank you, the reader, for your continuing support. Without you, I would have no reason to do this work. I may complain of migraines from trawling through microfilm, and nettle stings from wandering through badly tended graveyards, but I freely admit that I wouldn't have it any other way.

Also, without researching this book, I would have remained unaware of the striking and though provoking poetry of J.W Streets, and as such, would like to leave you with one of his finest works.

Thank you for reading.

The Dead: by J.W Streets; 1915.

Let music vast, triumphal, fill the world's great nave,
Voicing the peerless theme of noble youth
Who rose to Life's sublimest greatness at the grave
And won from Death the diadem of Truth!
No requiem solemn, funeral chant so drear
Ought mark their passing to the vast beyond
As at the shrine of Memory we revere,
Crooning their names in murmurings so fond!
For these like some great planet spheric- whirl'd
Have swung into the orbit of a greater world.

These topped the hill of Youth; stood on the verge
Of vision; saw within the furthest star
Spiritual presences, Love's own avatar;
These the twin worlds of soul and flesh did merge
Into a dream, a consciousness that stole
Around their spirits like an aureole.

Knew moments mad with ecstasy, when years
And dreams a happy bridal knew
In Life attained; when mystery that grew
Around the fringe of Life generating years
Was swept into the magic of a morn
From darkness filched, from Love Eternal born.

These flushed with hope; with star-uplifted eyes;
Strained and tense with consciousness of life;
Strung to high purpose; plumed for Youth's astral skies ;
These closed with Death in vast Olympian strife!
Laughed at the fate that lured them from their paradise
To fling their rapturous souls in deathless sacrifice!

Thus should we pay our tributary tears
When Youth doth triumph over Death; when he,
Mad with the promise of the future years,
Yieldeth his will and dies for Liberty?

When he, like some great eagle, lightning- wing'd,
Doth sweep above the dawn, the plains of light,
Winging swift passage (tho' by terror Ring'd)
And heedless plunge into the heart of night?
Why weep when Youth doth burst the prison of the clod
And rise unto the heritage, the greatness of a God?

Say not that these are dead: O rather say
That these do live (does nobleness e'er die?)
Who might have fled with Life's autumnal day
And ne'er .have left their soul unto posterity.
These nobly died: in that they live: their sin and vice
Thro' Honour purified became high sacrifice.

Perchance the years their purpose would have worn;
Bred hate, despair, and disillusionment;
Maybe their faith had melted into scorn
Till Life with tragic destinies was pent:
But in one hour of highest sacrifice
Poured out upon the altar-steps of Liberty
They consecrated Life-its destinies and vice-
And wrought within that hour their immortality.

Swell out the song of life since these are meet
In fields of fadeless Memory to play
Where Life and Love in happy bridals meet;
Where Spirits wed on earth
Their ecstasies of birth,
Embrace within the rapture of eternal day!
There, Father, thou canst greet thy son,
Aspiring to the greatness he hath won;
There, Mother, prostrate with your tears,
Within that spirit-heaven remote, afar,
Beyond the night of future years
Behold his soul a bright and fadeless Star!

Sob out no dirge for peerless nobleness,
For Youth triumphant, greater than his fate!
It is an hour when proud of soul, elate,
Man's greatness swells our little consciousness:
When on the wings of aspiration we do rise
And reach to God beyond the brazen skies.

There is a place beyond the bourne of Time,
A niche within the archives of Eternity,
Where souls that touched on earth a chord sublime
Dwell in concordant spirit-harmony:
There these repose who gave their love, their youth,
To feed the dying, sacred flame of Truth.

Theirs is the mighty music of the fadeless stars;
The chant of Life, exultant with high esctasy;
The strength of suffering gods who toil with many scars

To wrest promethean fire for dead humanity.
Beyond our ken, beyond the limit of the years
They sweep into the soul the freedom of the spheres.

Their life will burn with unextinguished flame
To other Youth who tread Life's upland way;
The lustre of their chivalry will shame
All drift of life into a comic play:

And growing Youth will look with wistful eyes
On unexampled manhood meeting death
With unexampled scorn and sacrifice,
Till to their mighty yearning there cometh
An inspiration to achieve and emulate
The youth who died Life's grandeur to perpetuate.

O Youth too great with Littleness to dwell!
O soul of Youth triumphant over death!
O envious manhood keeping sentinel
O'er nobleness of life! O oracle which saith:
'The soul of life is in the will to give:
The best to life in willing sacrifice:
Youth only reaches greatness when he dies
In fullest prime that love and truth may live.
Light's born in darkness, Life breaks from the tomb:
To never die and live, O dark and tragic doom!'

Index